METHODS OF
DYNAMIC ECONOMICS

METHODS OF DYNAMIC ECONOMICS

JOHN HICKS

CLARENDON PRESS · OXFORD

1985

Oxford University Press, Walton Street, Oxford OX2 6DP
Oxford New York Toronto
Delhi Bombay Calcutta Madras Karachi
Kuala Lumpur Singapore Hong Kong Tokyo
Nairobi Dar es Salaam Cape Town
Melbourne Auckland
and associated companies in
Beirut Berlin Ibadan Nicosia

Oxford is a trade mark of Oxford University Press

Published in the United States
by Oxford University Press, New York

British Library Cataloguing in Publication Data

Hicks, John, 1904–
Methods of dynamic economics.
1. Economic development—Mathematical models
I. Title
339.5'0724   HD75.5
ISBN 0–19–828530–2

Library of Congress Cataloging in Publication Data

Hicks, John Richard, Sir, 1904–
Methods of dynamic economics.

Includes index.
1. Economics. I. Title.
HB171.H6345   1985   330   85-15508
ISBN 0–19–828530–2

Set by Downdell Limited, Oxford
Printed in Great Britain at
the University Press, Oxford
by David Stanford
Printer to the University

PREFACE

The present volume is based upon one which I published in 1965, *Capital and Growth* (*CG*). To a large extent it is a new edition of the first Part of that work. The sub-title which I gave to that Part has been carried over to be the present title.

The reason why it has seemed suitable for a revision to take this form is the following. I had long been convinced that it was the First Part of *CG* that had the most value. The latter Parts, which were appended to it in *CG*, do not, with the exception of some passages, really belong. They are mostly no more than my own versions of work that had already been done by others. Not much attention has been paid to them; few people have found them interesting. That they have been bound up with Part I may well have reduced the number of readers which that might have had.

So I was not surprised when it was suggested to me that it would be good to bring out a new edition of the First Part separately, with what one began by thinking would be no more than a few minor adjustments, just enough to enable that Part to stand by itself. The idea was appealing; but when I got down to making those adjustments, I found that they had to be more than I had at first imagined. To rewrite those chapters in the light of all that has been done, by others, during these last twenty years, would have been a herculean task, quite beyond my capacity. There were nevertheless some things which I had done myself, during that time, which were to the point. I could not put out a new edition without giving them some recognition. Just to put in references to them would not have been enough. It would be better to work them in, even though that meant, in some cases, important changes.

The next book I published, after *CG*, was my *Critical Essays in Monetary Theory*. One of the bits of new work in that book was 'A Note on the Treatise' (Keynes's *Treatise on Money*). When I had finished it I saw that it could have provided a link between the Marshall chapter in *CG* and the 'post-Keynesian' chapters which followed it. So I have adapted it, and somewhat developed it, to appear as a new Chapter 6, 'The Methods of Keynes', fitting into that place in the present volume.

There are several pieces on Smith and Ricardo which I have published since 1965; most are included in the third volume of my *Collected Essays* (*Classics and Moderns*, 1983). They have put the old Chapter 4 of *CG* quite out of date. It has accordingly been replaced by a new Chapter 4, which has no more than a page or two in common with its predecessor.

A more formidable problem was set by *Capital and Time* (1973), a 'neo-Austrian' theory of capital which was not at all in my mind when *CG* was being written. When I had it, I saw that it was another *method* which ought to have been included. So I have made a sketch of it (it is no more than that) to appear here as Chapter 14.

But that showed up that there was a chapter in the old *CG*, in a part of that book which I was cutting out, which belonged. For like the method of *Capital and Time*, it was concerned with the ways in which a productive system can adjust itself to new techniques, when it is tied down by structural rigidities, as all actual economies surely are. It was concerned with 'horizontal' rigidities, while those of *Capital and Time* were 'vertical'. I doubt if much is known, even now, about what happens when (as in practice) both are present; still, it is helpful to have both in mind. So there is one chapter of this book (13), based on Chapter 16 of *CG*, which deals with the 'horizontal', to match Chapter 14.

I make no claim that, even with these additions, all possible 'methods of dynamic economics' have been covered. But I think that what emerges, after they have been brought in, is a better classification than that which emerged from the old Part I of *CG*.

There does not seem to be anything else, from the rest of *CG* (after Part I) which has a claim to inclusion. There is however one chapter, that on 'Optimum Saving', which I am reluctant to omit. It does not belong here, since it is not, in the sense of this book, *dynamic*. But it must not get lost. For it disposes, I think conclusively, of an error into which some very distinguished economists have fallen. So I have kept it in—as an Appendix.

CONTENTS

1

METHOD, DYNAMICS, AND STATICS

The terms which I have used in the title of this book require to be defined. What am I to mean by *method*? and what by *dynamics*?

A method, I shall find it convenient to say, is a family, or class, of models. A model is a piece of theory, a theoretical construction, which is intended to be applied to a certain range of facts. (There are several ways in which economic models are applied, which we shall be able to distinguish.) Models may thus be classified according the facts to which they are intended to refer; so we have models of international trade, of labour relations, of the money market, and so on. But a class of models, when the grouping was of this character, would not at all conveniently be called a *method*. The particular grouping which I have in mind relates to the dynamic character of the model. I think we shall find that for that kind of grouping the term *method* is appropriate.

What then is dynamics, Economic Dynamics? The definition of Economic Dynamics was for long a matter of controversy; but we need not be much troubled by those controversies here. It is easy enough, at this time of day, to see why there should have been various definitions. It was very natural that an author, approaching what before him was largely uncharted territory, should distinguish as *his* dynamics that stretch of it which lay immediately ahead of him on his own selected approach. (Then, when that strip had been colonized, the name would shift to the next strip that lay ahead.) Special definitions of that sort are abundant; they have been helpful, in their own places, as marks for the stages of some particular argument; but the meanings of dynamics which they give are not general meanings. The general meaning, which concerns us here, must be something more inclusive.

When we look for a general meaning it is not hard to see what it must be. There is a simple line of thought which impels us directly to it.

If there is one thing which dynamics must mean, which it cannot help meaning, it is 'not statics'. The definition of Economic Dynamics must follow from the definition of Economic Statics: when we have defined one we have defined the other.

The distinction between statics and dynamics is (of course) not originally an economic distinction. It is an echo of a far older distinction in mathematical mechanics; a reference to that older meaning will always be at the back of one's mind. It is a fault to allow oneself to become the victim of such analogies, but it is desirable, if we are to avoid confusion, to pay some attention to them.

It is undoubtedly true, in this case, that there cannot be a perfect fit. In mechanics, statics is concerned with rest, dynamics with motion; but no economic system is ever at rest in anything like the mechanical sense. Production is itself a process: by its very nature it is a process of change. All we can do is to define a static condition as one in which certain key variables (the quantities of commodities that are produced and consumed, and the prices at which they are exchanged) are unchanging. A dynamic condition is then, by inevitable opposition, one in which they are changing; and dynamic theory is the analysis of the processes by which they change.

This is in fact the definition of the scope of Economic Dynamics which I shall be using in the following chapters. It is obvious that it is a wide definition, which does not merely abstain from drawing a line between trend and fluctuation. It includes the study of change in particular markets as well as in the whole economy. It should deal with specialization and diversification as well as with 'growth'. It is indeed so wide that it may be suspected of being too wide. Will not dynamics, defined in this way, swallow up the whole of economics? Is any place left for Economic Statics?

I believe that there is a place for Economic Statics, quite an important place, though what it is requires some clearing up. Because our books start with statics, they take it much too much for granted. There is a good deal to be said about the scope (and method) of Economic Statics, and some of this I must inflict on the reader (in this chapter and in that which follows). We shall not be in a proper position to discuss dynamics until we are really clear about statics. If dynamics is 'not statics', then by deepening our conception of statics we are (by implication) deepening our conception of dynamics also.

The static–dynamic distinction looks rather different according to the kind of economic theory where it is used. It is rather different in Welfare Economics from what it is in Positive Economics, and (as we shall see) in different kinds of Positive Economics. It will be useful to look at it as it appears in these various fields, and perhaps to clear our ideas about the relations between these fields, just a little, as we go along.

I begin with Welfare Economics. It is only too obvious that most traditional Welfare Economics—whether of the 'old' (Pigouvian) or of the 'new' variety—has in fact been static. It has assumed that wants are constant, and resources are constant; it has then inquired into the characteristics of 'optimum' organization, of the organization which, according to some conception of 'best', will satisfy these wants in the 'best' way. It was no doubt necessary to begin in that manner, since the problems that arise, even at that stage, are difficult enough. The static assumption is a simplification which makes the problem more tractable, so that some progress can be made with it, as could hardly be made if the full complexities of a changing economy were faced at the start. Concentration upon static Welfare Economics has, however, proved to be quite dangerous. Though many of the static welfare problems are real problems, and many of the static 'solutions' give a guide to real solutions, which will persist however the welfare problem is dynamized, that is not always true. It is important (and it is increasingly realized to be important) to rethink the welfare problem in terms of a changing economy, in which resources (at least) are varying, either 'autonomously' or as a consequence of present behaviour. And, when one looks at them in that light, some of the 'welfare' conclusions look quite a bit different. Permanent and temporary gains (and losses) would have to be distinguished.

In principle, then, in the welfare field statics is just a preliminary to dynamics, a preliminary which it was no doubt necessary to explore before proceeding to dynamic complications, but whose ultimate destination looks like being for a role which will be mainly pedagogic. That, however, may be going too far. For the dynamic complications are great, and are very hard to handle; thus, whenever it can be shown that, in relation to some particular problem, they are unimportant, it may be justifiable to neglect them. But often (one fears) one will not be able to show, only to guess, that they are unimportant: different people will guess in different ways.

———————

Let us, however, on the way to our next topic, that of Positive Economics, consider a case in which Static Welfare Economics has at least thrown up interesting subjects for discussion. This is in the analysis of industrial structure (monopoly and competition). Here we have both a welfare problem and a positive-economic problem: we are contrasting the welfare optimum (or a welfare optimum) with the (possibly or probably) non-optimum position thrown up by some 'actual' organization. The welfare term in this comparison is relatively clear (or at least we may say that its ambiguities are by now well understood); but on the 'actual' side there is a distinction, which cries out to be made, but which is in fact too often overlooked.

What we may be doing is to compare the optimum position (that which *would* be achieved if wants were satisfied 'best' on some criterion) with the position which *would* be realized if the economy were organized on some given principle: such as profit maximization without collusion, profit maximization with a certain kind of collusion, normal cost pricing, discriminatory pricing, and so on. To what extent, we may ask, will the distribution of resources that is established under one of these systems, or market forms, approximate to, or depart from, the welfare optimum as above defined? (This includes, of course, the question whether organization, on the principle that is under examination, is possible at all.) All these questions, it should be noticed, are theoretical questions, like the welfare questions. They cannot be answered by an appeal to facts. The most that facts can do is to throw some indirect light upon them.

Contrasted with these is the much more empirical problem, in which we are concerned with actual behaviour, trying to make sense of actual data, coming (as actual data have to come) from some particular time and place. We can then test out upon them, as hypotheses, the maximum profit hypothesis, the full cost hypothesis, or any other that one can think up; we must, however, be prepared to find that the principles (if they can be called such) on which the actual economy which we are examining is run are very mixed. The most that we can expect is that there will be an approximation to one or other of the standard types of organization. If so, we can use the results that we have derived from a study of these types to judge (in terms of departure from the welfare optimum) the actual organization, at the particular time, of the particular economy. If not so, we may only be able to judge it when we have invented a new type, and constructed the new theory (simple or complicated) which belongs to it.

It seems to be suggested by this example (it is only an example) that Positive Economics has a 'pure' branch as well as an 'applied' branch, and that it is important to distinguish them. Welfare Economics is pure economics, but it is not the only part of pure economics. A considerable part of economic theory is not Welfare Economics: but, like Welfare Economics, it is pure theory, not tied down to particular time and place.

In setting against this pure branch an applied branch I do not mean to imply that the applied branch is non-theoretical. For one of the major constituents of the applied branch is econometrics. Econometric hypotheses (or models) are meant to be checked against facts, so that they belong to the applied branch; but they appear, at least on the surface, to be quite as theoretical in character as the models of 'pure' theory. The one kind can indeed quite easily be mistaken for the other. It may indeed be true that in the beginning they were hardly differentiated. It was then not evident that Pure Positive Economics offered any choice of model; the task of the econometrist could then be thought to be confined to the 'fitting' of a model, given to him by the theorist, to the facts—indeed to any facts. But as time has gone on (and perhaps also as econometricians have become more ambitious) it has become apparent that this is not at all precisely what they have to do. The econometric model is to be fitted to *particular* facts—to US data over a certain period, or something like that. Its object is to explain the working of that economy (or of some aspect of that economy) in the simplest possible terms. The wise econometrist will accordingly use his general knowledge of that economy to select 'strategic factors' which seem likely to be important, so that they must be incorporated into his model; and to reject things which, on general knowledge, seem unlikely to be important in that case. (He does, of course, have methods by which he can test the desirability of including such factors as, on general knowledge, seem to be on the margin of doubt.) But he can hardly proceed at all without some hunch about the kinds of things he is going to include.

Econometric models of this sort are very important; I have no desire to depreciate them. But I would insist that they are not the only sort of positive model that we need.

For there is another kind of question which we may properly ask, which is not a normative, or 'welfare', question, and not an econometric question. Instead of asking, like the econometrists, how *did* such and such an economy work, over such and such a past period, we may ask—what would be the working of an economy, which was constructed on given lines, whether an economy of that sort has actually existed or not? This is a purely theoretical question, like the welfare question: it cannot be answered by an appeal to facts. Nor can the answer be tested by an appeal to facts, save in special cases, where we may be able to find an economy that looks as if its working should be interpretable in terms of the prescribed rules. We can then perhaps test the hypothesis that this is so. Some of the answers to questions that are of this sort may be testable to that extent, but certainly not all. Yet, among those that are untestable, there are some to which we should much like to have some kind of answer.[1]

That Pure Positive Theory of this sort is necessary, is (I think) made apparent by the 'monopoly-competition' example given above. When the economist has got his 'welfare' rules and has established (if he can) that existing organization does not satisfy them, he has still not finished his job. For he has no right to criticize the existing organization simply on account of what he has so far shown. For anything that is yet apparent it may be that there is no *practicable* organization which will satisfy wants any 'better', which will approach the optimum any more nearly. In order to have a basis for criticism it has to be shown that there is a practicable alternative organization which can be expected to do this. But that alternative organization (by definition) does not yet exist; its properties cannot be established, at least in general, by econometric methods. They can only be perceived, however dimly, by theoretical inquiry–by what I am calling Pure Positive Economics.[2]

I return to statics—and dynamics. The status of statics in Pure Positive Theory is not very different from what it is in Welfare Economics —as is not surprising, in view of the strictly theoretical character of both branches. Here, as in Welfare Economics, if we begin with statics we do so because it is easier. Again, as in Welfare Economics, there may be some cases where static analysis gives us all that we

---

[1] Thus, when what we are doing is Pure Positive Economics, we should not allow ourselves to be bullied by those who insist that all our concepts must be 'operationally meaningful'. That demand is fair enough, if we are doing econometrics, or preparing theory for the econometrist; but it is not fair if we have a different intention.

[2] It may be observed, in passing, that the characteristic of econometrics which we have been discussing—that its theory is applied theory, not pure theory—explains why it is that it can only lead up to 'projections' or prognostications: forecasts of what will happen, if the same forces as have been operating continue to operate in the future, not what will happen if a new form of organization (in the widest sense) is introduced. Once 'policy' is introduced as a variable, we have to go beyond econometrics.

require, so that we can rest without going further. But there are others—as we learn more they become increasingly frequent—where we cannot get all that we need by the use of static methods, or where the use of static method is seriously misleading. It then becomes necessary to push on into dynamic territory; the sorting out of the problems that then arise—in Pure Positive Economics—will be the main subject of the later chapters of this book.

But before we come to that let us look at the position on the applied side, which we shall find to be appreciably different. Statics, here, is not a mere preliminary to dynamics: it has an independent status of its own. There exist applied problems which, by their nature, are purely static. For the study of such problems static analysis requires to be elaborated much more fully than it would have to be if its role were no more than that of a preliminary.

Take, as a simple example, the question: why are Englishmen, on the average, richer than (say) Greeks? This is quite a normal question of applied economics, and as such it must of course have a time reference; it refers (obviously) to Englishmen and Greeks in the twentieth century AD and not to any earlier period of history. The particular date of reference is not, however, of much importance: one would not mind too much if the figures on which one was commenting were 1955 figures for one country and 1960 figures for the other. The question is one about the *states* of the economies in question, not about any process of change. Questions such as this (and there are very many such questions which concern economists) are static questions: it ought to be possible to deal with them without going outside static theory.

Accordingly, in applied economics, there is nothing unrealistic about statics: the line between statics and dynamics is not a line between abstraction and realism. It may indeed be noticed (as a confirmation) that a similar distinction appears in the wholly realistic field of economic history. One of the standard ways of writing economic history (much practised by political historians in their economic chapters) is to survey the state of the economy under consideration, as it was in various historical periods, comparing one state with another. This is comparative statics. It is when the economic historian tries to throw his work into the form of a narrative that it becomes, in our sense, dynamic. And any examination of the work of economic historians will show what a difficult threshold has to be crossed at that point.

Static problems, then, are real problems, but static theory is a matter of static method, and that is rather a different matter. By the *state* of a given economy one would appear to mean its average performance over a fairly long period, short-run fluctuations being cancelled out. Since one was not interested in short-run fluctuations it would seem to be adequate to represent the economy by a model which was in this average condition throughout the whole of the period; so that it was in a static condition, as we have been using the term. This is the way in which static models are used, and I think must be used, for appropriate purposes in applied economics. The model exhibits an unchanging economy, although it is to be applied to the study of an economy which is in fact in a condition of change.

So far as that one must go; but the ground on which one is treading is already beginning to be treacherous. Suppose, to take a simple but (as it turns out) most important case, that the actual economy being studied is in fact a progressive economy, in the sense that it is accumulating real capital, having (in some sense) more real equipment at the end of the period under consideration than it had at the beginning. We have then to do considerable violence to it if we are to fit it into a static model. We must replace its actual (changing) stock of capital by a constant stock of capital, not (in strictness) the capital that it had at the beginning of the period, but its average capital over the period. But if we do that, what do we do about investment? There is no difficulty about the part of the investment which makes good the wastage of capital; such replacement investment is entirely consistent with a static model. But the net investment, which increases the capital stock, cannot be shown as increasing the capital stock. It is, of course, a part of production, and will have to be shown as part of the social product. The point is that it cannot be distinguished, as investment, from other parts of the social product. In statics, consumption goods and investment goods are just things that are produced: there is no economic difference between them, save the ordinary imperfect substitutability by which any sort of good differs from another.

Consider, as an illustration of this principle, the question of distribution among factors. There is no obvious reason why this should not be treated as a static problem; it is certainly capable of being formulated in static terms. Suppose we take the particular question: why is the share of (say) rent in the British National Income lower in the twentieth century than in the eighteenth? (I take a case where the fact is pretty indubitable.) We are clearly then asking a question about states, not about processes, so that it seems to call for treatment on static lines. It then follows at once from the general characteristics of static analysis, just elucidated, that we must not expect to find an explanation of the change in question in any of the things that are excluded from static analysis—as for instance anything to do with saving and investment (as such). All that could possibly be relevant in this direction (I do not say that it would be important in this particular case) is a change in the characteristics of the particular sorts of consumption and investment goods being produced in the periods under consideration; a change in the proportion of much-land-using goods, for instance, in the whole national product (consumption goods and investment goods together). It is only in this sense (so long as we consider the problem statically) that anything to do with saving and investment can possibly be relevant.

Nevertheless, once it is realized that we have to do this kind of violence to the facts in fitting them to a static model, so that we are compelled by our method to leave out things which may well be relevant, the question emerges: cannot we find a way of doing better? If the economy with which we are dealing (or even one only of the economies which we are comparing) is in fact a progressive economy, it may be claimed that its progressiveness is one of its characteristics: that it is in a *state* of progress, or growth. Even though we are only concerned with its average performance over the period, its average growth rate over the period is a part of that average performance.

It was, I believe, first shown by Cassel[3] that a model of steady growth can be constructed which can be handled in much the same way as the static model. Through the work of Harrod, Domar, Joan Robinson, Kaldor, and many others, the use of such a 'steady state model' has become familiar. This is a tool that can be used in various ways; so it surely is fair to regard it, and the uses that are made of it, as constituting a 'method', in the sense that was explained at the beginning of this chapter. But is it a dynamic method? It is on the edge between statics and dynamics: it is dynamic if one looks at it one way, static if one looks at it another. If it is just used for comparison between states, even though they are progressive states, then I (now) think we should reckon it to be used in a static manner. But if we use it as a standard of reference, with which performances that are not so uniform are being compared, it is an ingredient in a dynamic theory,

---

[3] *Theory of Social Economy*, ch. 1, sect. 6. It may be that Cassel was developing a suggestion of Marshall's (see below, p. 44).

so that the use we make of it is dynamic. A particular case of this is the problem of Traverse, of the existence of a path from one steady state to another, which will receive some attention to Chapters 13–14 below.[4]

[4] I have changed my mind on this matter of classification since I wrote *Capital and Growth*. I there reckoned the 'Growth Equilibrium Method', as I called it, to be one of the dynamic methods which I identified. I now feel it to be clearer, and more convenient, to classify otherwise.

This is in part a consequence of events. In the 'golden age' of the sixties, as it appears in retrospect, a steady-state model seemed often to be acceptable as an approximation to reality: in the darker days that have followed it is less appealing.

2

THE CONCEPT OF EQUILIBRIUM

There is one further matter, not specially belonging to dynamic theory, on which something must be said before we start on dynamics. What is the meaning which we are to give to the concept of 'equilibrium'? In statics, equilibrium is fundamental; in dynamics, as we shall find, we cannot do without it; but even in statics it is treacherous, and in dynamics unless we are very careful, it will trip us up completely. It is inevitable that we should build our concept of dynamic equilibrium on the more familiar conception of equilibrium in statics. It will be wise to begin by getting the static foundation as firm as we can.

Like 'statics' and 'dynamics' themselves, 'equilibrium' is a borrowing from mathematical mechanics; but it is a question whether the mechanical and economic concepts of 'equilibrium' have much more than a name in common. The static equilibrium of mechanics is a balance of forces; but though economists began by thinking of their static equilibrium as a balance of forces—as, for instance, the 'forces' of supply and demand—that is a very poor account of what the static equilibrium of economics means. Attempts have been made (most notably by Samuelson, in his *Foundations of Economic Analysis*[1]) to find a closer association at a deeper level; but I have myself come to doubt whether they give us much help. It is safer, in my view, to define the static equilibrium of economics as an independent concept in its own right.

The static economy (in which wants are unchanging, and resources unchanging) is in a state of equilibrium when all the 'individuals' in it are choosing those quantities, which, out of the alternatives available to them, they prefer to produce and to consume. (*Individuals* is to be taken in a wide sense, to include any units, as for instance firms, to which we attribute some freedom of independent choice: *preference* is interpreted to mean maximizing something—whether objective [profit] or subjective [utility] does not here matter.) The alternatives that are open are set in part by *external constraints* (which

[1] Especially ch. 9.

may be differently defined, according as we select the data of a particular problem, but must generally include the supplies of land and of physical capital, and the state of technology); these, in a static economy, must be taken to be constant. But they are also set in large part by the choices made by other 'individuals'; and the way in which the choices made by 'individuals' set constraints on the choices made by other 'individuals' will differ from one market form (or more generally from one type of economic organization) to another.[2]

The crucial assumption of static theory (without which it could not have been developed as it has been developed) is that a static economy (static, because tastes and resources are unchanging) can be treated as if it were in equilibrium: the quantities produced and consumed will be (near enough) the equilibrium quantities that have just been described. Economists are so used to this equilibrium assumption that they are inclined to take it for granted; for present purposes, however, we must not let it slip by without noticing it.

Even if we do not make the equilibrium assumption, there are some properties of the static economy which can be established. Even without it, we can write down certain relations ('social accounting identities'), of which equality between demand and supply in any market (in the sense of actual quantity bought and actual quantity sold) may be regarded as typical. It is not to be denied that these relations, in themselves, give us a certain insight into the structure of the economy; but they are of little use for comparative purposes. For such purposes (to take the simplest illustration) the demand and supply, which are necessarily equal as an identity, have to be reinterpreted as a point of intersection on demand and supply schedules; and for the construction of such schedules (as for the construction of the more complicated functions which play the same role in the study of inter-related markets) we require the equilibrium assumption. It is essential for *comparative* statics that the quantities chosen can be taken to be equilibrium quantities.

But because we need the equilibrium assumption, it does not follow that we have a right to it. And indeed, as soon as we allow ourselves to question it, it becomes obvious that it needs much justification. There is much to be said about it, even on the static level; but to go into it at

---

[2] That we do have some freedom on what constraints shall be treated as external constraints is made evident by the case of the national economy. When we are considering it by itself, we treat the trading opportunities open to it as external constraints; but when we treat it as part of the international economy, these must be taken as consequences of the choices of other 'individuals'.

all fully would draw us aside from our main task. There are just a few things (which, as we shall see, have dynamic counterparts) that must be said.

It has first to be noticed that the equilibrium assumption looks distinctly different, according as it is used in one or another of the three branches of economic theory (even confining attention to the static departments of those three branches) that were distinguished in Chapter 1.

In Welfare Economics there is no problem: the equilibrium assumption is included in the way the theory is set up. This is certainly so if we define our social optimum by some sort of 'social welfare function'; for if we do that we are treating the economy *as if* it consisted of a single 'individual': it is the equilibrium choice of that single chooser which *is* the optimum choice. And the position does not seem to be radically different if we insist on pluralism, as for instance when we 'reconcile' the maximization of utility by distinct 'individuals' by compensation devices, so long as the maximization of utility by each individual is kept as *one* of the conditions of optimization. A static welfare optimum has to be an equilibrium.

It is in Positive Economics that there is a problem; but it is a different problem in the pure from what it is in the applied branch.

In Pure Positive Economics (where, as will be remembered, we assume a *given* type of organization) it is necessary, if the equilibrium assumption is to be justified, that we should be able to assert the existence of a *tendency* to equilibrium; and indeed, if the assumption is to be usable, it must be a strong tendency. There are several questions here to be distinguished.

In the first place it is by no means inevitable, in an arbitrarily given form of organization, that an equilibrium should exist at all. In the simple cases with which we are most familiar (such as the Marshallian case of a single industry—the production of a single product considered in isolation) there may be no doubt about it; but even there we have to be careful. There is no question, in the case of the single market, that under perfect competition, under monopoly, and under imperfect competition without oligopoly, equilibrium does exist; but one has only to point to the tortured history of duopoly theory to show that there are market forms, not necessarily unrealistic or unimportant, where the mere existence of equilibrium, even in a single market, is doubtful. In the case of the whole (closed) economy, it is only quite recently that the necessary existence of an equilibrium has been established, even for the simplest form of organization, that in which perfect competition is taken for granted.[3] For what forms of imperfect competition (if there are any) a similar necessity can be established is still (I believe) an open question.

But let that pass. Even if the equilibrium exists, it has still to be shown that there is a tendency towards it. This, as Samuelson has (rightly) emphasized, is not a matter that can be settled, once and for all, as soon as the type of economic organization (according to the usual *static* classification) has been decided. A perfectly competitive system, for instance, may have a strong tendency to equilibrium, or it may not. The simplest example of this (sufficient to establish the point) is the 'cobweb theorem'. Even in the single market, under perfect competition, and such that the existence of equilibrium is indubitable, there may be no *tendency* to equilibrium, if speeds of reaction to price change are perverse. Something has to be specified about reactions to disequilibrium before the existence of a tendency to equilibrium can be asserted. The tendency to (static) equilibrium is itself a dynamic matter.[4]

[3] An outline of the proof, and of the steps by which it was accomplished, is given in Dorfman, Samuelson, and Solow, *Linear Programming and Economic Analysis*, pp. 366 ff. A still briefer outline, which does still (I think) bring out the main points, is given in my 'Survey of Linear Theory' (*Economic Journal*, December 1960). This is reprinted in my *Collected Essays* III.

[4] A word may usefully be inserted here (though it can do no more than skirt the fringe of a large subject) about the relation between this tendency to equilibrium and the stability of equilibrium, which has been intensively treated by mathematical economists. There is just one point that I want to make; and I shall only take the simplest case in which it arises.

In a perfectly competitive market, an ordinary downward-sloping demand curve for a product (say a farm product) may be confronted with a 'backward-sloping' supply curve—because (to follow the old story) farmers consume more of their own product when they can satisfy their rudimentary demands for the products of urban industry more easily. Supply and demand curves may then have multiple intersections, of which some (so we are informed by the textbooks) are 'unstable'. What exactly does this mean?

The property (it will be noticed) is a purely static property: it can be read off from the diagram, without any information about speeds of reaction, or anything about patterns of reaction that cannot be expressed in static terms. (If we did have information about speeds of reaction, we might find, on 'cobweb' lines, that some of the 'statically stable' positions were in fact unstable.) What is it that distinguishes the 'statically unstable' position (or positions) in the absence of such information?

The 'statically unstable' position is itself an equilibrium: if it were hit upon, buyers and sellers would be making the offers which they preferred, at the price in question, and these offers would fit together. The only thing which can distinguish it from a

Let that pass again. Even if the equilibrium exists, and the tendency to equilibrium exists, we may still have insufficient ground to justify the equilibrium assumption if the convergence to equilibrium is very slow. For then, in any period of reasonable length that begins from a position which is out of equilibrium, the time that is occupied in approaching equilibrium (and still remaining, perhaps, quite far away from it) will be long in proportion to the length of the later phase, in which an equilibrium position is (approximately) realized. It is true that we can always, in a sense, overcome this last difficulty by lengthening the period of time for which tastes and resources are to be kept static; but static comparisons, which relate to average states over very long periods of time, will not often be very interesting.

There is, however, an alternative procedure which in such cases one would expect to be more promising. It will be remembered that we have some liberty to select the constraints which, in a particular model, are to be treated as *external*; or, what comes to the same thing, that we have some liberty to specify the choices which are to be regarded as 'open' choices, so that to them the equilibrium assumption is to be applied. If, with respect to some particular choices, convergence to equilibrium is very slow, it may be better not to regard such choices as open choices. What we then get is a less 'general' or less 'full' equilibrium than we should have got if we had left them open; it may nevertheless be more interesting and more useful.

An obvious example of this device is Marshall's 'short-period equilibrium', in which the fixed equipment of the (single industry) economy is kept constant; choices that relate to the structure and to

---

'statically stable' position is that it is an equilibrium which can only be reached *by accident*. If there is any rule for the correction of disequilibrium positions—so long as that rule incorporates the merely *directional* provision that the price is to be raised when demand exceeds supply, lowered when supply exceeds demand—it will not be possible for the statically unstable position to be reached as the terminus of a process of adjustment. A correction of a disequilibrium position in its neighbourhood will always lead *away* from it.

By this distinction the contrast between the 'statically stable' and 'statically unstable' position is (I think) made clear. It is not true that *any* rule of adjustment, which incorporates the directional provision, must lead to a 'statically stable' position; for the rule may be such (as in the case of the 'explosive cobweb') that every correction that is made, though it is the 'right' direction, will always overshoot the mark. What is true is that the statically unstable position cannot be reached by any such correction, since the correction goes, in principle, the wrong way. It can be hit upon by accident, but not by a process of correction, so long as that process has the merely directional provision in it.

I believe that this argument can be generalized to cover cases of multiple markets; but I shall not go into that here.

the size of that equipment are not, within the 'short-period' model, regarded as being 'open'. But it is not hard to find other examples; and (as we shall see when we come back to it in Chapter 5) Marshall's device has other aspects which will concern us very seriously, as well as this.

――――――――

It is the Pure Positive branch of Economic Dynamics which will be our main concern in the following chapters: the main thing that is still to be done in this is to commence consideration of the equilibrium concept in that territory. But before proceeding to that topic, a word should be inserted about the remaining branch of static theory, the 'applied' branch.

This, it will be remembered, is theory that is to be applied to actual facts: to the performance of an actual economy over a particular historical period. The form of organization that is assumed is chosen to fit those facts; it is not examined for its own sake, for its intrinsic intellectual interest or as an organization that might be brought into being in conditions that we wish to suppose. Here, then, it can only be a question of applying the equilibrium concept to such choices as, in the particular economy under consideration, may reasonably be regarded as 'open': these, in some economies, may have quite a restricted scope. (We may, and commonly do, limit it still further in the interest of simplification.) But whether the scope of the open choices is wide or narrow, we are here committed, by the mere decision to apply a static model, to the choice of a model which satisfies the requirements that we have been laying down. The equilibrium must exist, and there must be a tendency to it; if these conditions do not hold in the model that has been selected, it cannot be used for the static analysis of the facts in question, and must be rejected. A model which satisfies these conditions must be found.

The actual fitting of the model to the facts is a statistical (or econometric) question with which we are not here concerned. It is nevertheless important, even from our present point of view, to emphasize that the actual data, to which the static model is to be fitted, will not themselves be static. Even if we take the existence and stability of the model equilibrium for granted, we have still to ask how far the actual observed averages can be expected to correspond with the stationary values of the equilibrium model.

There are two questions here. One (the less important) is a matter of averaging. Consider the following illustration:

Let y_t be an index of production at time t. We are fitting a production function, so that y_t is supposed to be a function of quantities of factors of production, which at time t may be written x_{it} ($i = 1, 2, ..., m$). If this function were a linear function, such as

$$y_t = \sum_i a_i x_{it} + b$$

(a s and b constant), we could sum over time and take a mean value, giving

$$\text{mean } y = \sum_i a_i (\text{mean } x_i) + b$$

so that there would be the same relation between the mean y and the means of the x s as we should have got if the x s had been constant at their mean values. But if the function is not linear, this is not so. If it is log-linear (as with the Cobb–Douglas function)

$$\log y_t = \sum_i a_i \log x_{it} + b$$

the same procedure will give a relation between means of logs; and mean $\log y_t$ is the log of the geometric mean of the y s, so that the relation only comes out right if we take geometric means as our averages.

This is not to say that one mean is better than the other; the point is that averaging is itself a source of error, greater (of course) if the data (which are being treated as constant, though they are not constant) are in fact varying a good deal during the period under consideration. There is nothing surprising about that, but it is one thing to be remembered.

The more important question concerns the tendency to equilibrium. What exactly, when the data are changing, is this to be taken to mean? A natural interpretation would be something as follows.

Suppose that y_t^* is the equilibrium value of the variable y at time t, depending on parameters x_{it} as before. But now suppose that the actual value of y_t does not necessarily equal y_t^* but is merely drawn towards it, from its preceding value. We might then write

$$y_t - y_{t-1} = k(y_t^* - y_{t-1})$$

so that if $k = 1$ we have instantaneous adjustment, while if $k < 1$, there is only a tendency to equilibrium.

There is of course no reason in general why k should not be variable; but it is rather instructive to see what happens in the simplest case when it does not vary. Then, if we sum over n periods, and divide by n, we have

$$\frac{y_n - y_0}{n} = k \left(\text{mean } y_t^* - \text{mean } y_{t-1} \right)$$

$$= k \left(\text{mean } y_t^* - \text{mean } y_t \right) + \frac{y_n - y_0}{n} \ ,$$

so that $\text{mean } y_t^* - \text{mean } y_t = \dfrac{1-k}{k} \cdot \dfrac{y_n - y_0}{n} \ .$

It follows that there is no discrepancy, either if $k = 1$ (so that there is instantaneous adjustment), or if $y_n = y_0$ (so that the end value is the same as the initial value). If k is much less than unity, and if the economy is (say) an expanding economy, with y_n much larger than y_0, there may be a considerable discrepancy. The observed average is brought below the equilibrium average because of the *lag*.

With this last illustration, simple though it is, we are well on the way to dynamics. For suppose that instead of concentrating attention, as we have so far been doing, on the *average* performance of the economy during the n periods that have just been considered, we face up to the variations that occur in the course of those n periods, and bring them in as part of the phenomenon we are concerned to understand and explain. It would be possible to proceed as we have just been proceeding; and (as we shall see in more detail in the next chapter and in some of those that follow it) this is in fact the kind of procedure that is implied in the older work on Economic Dynamics, and in some (even) of the contemporary work. For reasons which I shall explain, I am myself convinced that this procedure is inadequate. But it does already throw up some of the problems of equilibrium in dynamics; it is a *half-way house* with which we shall in fact have to be much concerned.

We have found ourselves, in the course of our attempt to find a theoretical basis for the fitting of a static model to changing data, having to interpret that model in the sense of making equilibrium values of time t dependent upon parameters that belong to time t, and upon those parameters only. Yet we have found that in the *actual* process, values at time t do not so depend. There is a 'moving equilibrium'; but actual values are 'lagged' behind the equilibrium values. Thus we have (1) a set of rules by which the equilibrium values depend upon the parameters, and (2) a distinct set of rules by which the actual values are drawn towards the equilibrium values. This is the same kind of distinction as we found ourselves making when we were considering the *tendency* to a static equilibrium (in the Pure Positive static theory); it begins to look as if some such distinction is going to persist right through the dynamic field.

But what are these equilibrium values? I began with the assertion that there is equilibrium when all 'individuals' are choosing the quantities, to produce and to consume, which they prefer. To a conception of equilibrium that is of this type we must hold fast. But how can we make these quantities dependent (in a dynamic economy) upon current parameters—the equilibrium values of time t upon the parameters of time t—and upon those only? The question did not arise in a static model, since the parameters, on which the equilibrium depended, were at all dates the same. Here they are not the same. If (say) population is increasing, an 'equilibrium' that is based upon present population, paying no attention to the increase of population, will not even be a transitory equilibrium; there will be no reason why the 'individuals' should leave the population movement out of account in their investment decisions; there will be no reason why there should be even a 'tendency' in the direction of an equilibrium that is solely based upon present population. Similarly for other variables. The static equilibrium, entirely based upon current parameters, is in strictness irrelevant to the dynamic process.

That is why the picture of actual values chasing a 'moving equilibrium' (the equilibrium values of which are determined statically) has to be abandoned. There was a stage in the development of dynamic theory when it was a tempting picture; but it will not do. As soon as we face the problem of analysing a process, even its equilibrium values must be determined, somehow or other, in relation to the process. But how is this to be done?

The process is a process in time; time goes only one way. Past and future must be distinguished. Parameters that refer to the past, and those that refer to the future, each may enter into the determination of equilibrium values, but they will do so in different ways. The past, so far as it is relevant, is embodied in the *results* of past decisions: the physical capital of the economy and the acquired skills of labour.[5]

---

[5] It may be necessary, for some purposes, to allow for 'learning by experience'—the influence of past experience upon expectations of the future. This is another way in which past parameters may come in, or be brought in.

Instead of introducing past parameters explicitly, we can use the current resources that embody them. But the future is also relevant, and the future has no such *current* representative. We must introduce expectations of the future, of the future after time t, if the equilibrium values of time t are to be properly determined.

Expectations may be wrong or right; this simple consideration has a vital effect upon the kind of equilibrium concept (or concepts) that we require in dynamics. We need (1) *equilibrium at a point of time*; the system is in equilibrium in this sense if 'individuals' are reaching a preferred position, with respect to their expectations, as they are at that point. It is only to such an equilibrium that there can be a tendency. We also need (2) *equilibrium over a period of time*. If there is to be equilibrium over a period there must be equilibrium at every point of time within the period—an equilibrium which is of course based, as every point-of-time equilibrium must be based, upon its own expectations. But for period equilibrium there is the additional condition that these expectations must be consistent with one another and with what actually happens within the period. Period equilibrium is essential, in dynamic theory, as a standard of reference; but it is hard to see how there can, in general, be any 'tendency' to it.

The relation between the two conceptions can be spelled out in more detail as follows. Suppose that at t_1 (a point of time) there is 'point-of-time equilibrium'. It must be based upon expectations of the movement of parameters, some of which belong to the *period* t_1 to t_2, some of which belong after t_2. Suppose that at t_2 (the end of the period) there is again point-of-time equilibrium, based (of course) upon expectations of movement after t_2. If their expectations (about *post-t_2*) are different at t_2 from what they were at t_1, it will appear that the expectations of t_1 were wrong. So that although the system was in point-of-time equilibrium at t_1 *ex ante*, it does not appear to *have been* in point-of-time equilibrium at t_1, when it is looked at from t_2, *ex post*. And if actual events between t_1 and t_2 were different from what was expected at t_1, these t_1 expectations will similarly be shown to be wrong.[6] What this means is that from the point of view of

---

[6] There is indeed a fundamental difference between what happens to the *post-t_2* expectations, between t_1 and t_2, and what happens to the t_1–t_2 expectations. The former still relate to the future, at t_2 as at t_1, but the latter (at t_2) have been converted into facts. Expectations may (and probably will) be uncertain: there is nothing that has here been said about *point-of-time equilibrium* which makes it necessary that they should be certain. But for period equilibrium expectations that relate *within the period* will have to be certain. This may seem awkward, but I think it has to be faced. After all, it

t_2, the system was not in point-of-time equilibrium at t_1, nor on the course between t_1 and t_2. In order that there should be equilibrium *over the period*, there must be equilibrium at every point within the period, looked at both ways.

Static equilibrium is of course, by necessity, equilibrium over time; but there are other interesting examples of equilibrium over time that are not static. One is the steady state equilibrium to which allusion was made at the end of Chapter 1. More generally, every optimum path must be in equilibrium over time. It may indeed be said—it is not inconsistent with the proposed terminology that we should allow ourselves to say—that every path which is in equilibrium over time is an optimum path, under the 'constraint' of the particular organization that it assumes; but a path which was in equilibrium over time, under a non-optimum (say a monopolistically exploitative) form of organization, would not be an optimum path in a more general sense.

Some such distinctions as we have been making in this chapter seem to be unavoidable if we are to tidy up what has been a very untidy matter; but it is not to be denied that they can themselves be confusing. It is only by using them (as I plan to do in subsequent chapters) that we can really get them straight. But I may conclude this chapter by giving some preliminary warnings.

The temporal distinction which we have just been making (equilibrium *at a point of time* and equilibrium *over a period of time*) looks very like 'short period–long period', the Marshallian distinction that is so familiar. But it is not at all the same thing. The Marshallian distinction (as explained) belongs to the class of 'restricted-full' distinctions—a type of distinction which is valid, even in statics, where the temporal distinction does not occur. There is of course no reason why 'restricted-full' distinctions should not be made in dynamics also; the choices which we regard as 'open' may still be restricted, for particular purposes, in suitable ways.

It is indeed true that a restricted equilibrium, which is not a full equilibrium, becomes a disequilibrium position, from the point of view of the 'fuller' analysis, where the restriction has been removed. (The short-period equilibrium, which is not a long-period equilibrium, is a disequilibrium, from the point of view of the long period.)

---

enables us to say that risk and uncertainty are one of the causes of period disequilibrium; and that is one of the things which we shall want to say.

I shall be returning to this matter in Chapter 7.

And it is similarly true that an equilibrium at a point of time, which is not an equilibrium over the period in which that point of time occurs, is a disequilibrium position from the point of view of the period. (It is better to say that the path on which the disequilibrium position occurs is not an equilibrium path, over the period.) But an equilibrium over time may still be a restricted equilibrium. So far as the 'open' choices are concerned, there is equilibrium over time; but not all choices that might be open (or that we might want to consider as being open) are open. A full (or fuller) equilibrium may still have to be considered.

This last point has a particular bearing upon Welfare Economics (or Optimum theory). As was stated at the beginning of this chapter, a static welfare optimum has to be an equilibrium; we now see that the same must be true of a welfare optimum, in dynamics as in statics. It is nevertheless still possible (in both statics and dynamics) to distinguish between a restricted optimum and a full (or fuller) optimum. The distinction is the same as that between a restricted and a full equilibrium: the restricted optimum is a restricted equilibrium, and the full optimum is a full equilibrium. From the point of view of the full equilibrium (or optimum) the restricted optimum is not an equilibrium. It is an equilibrium, subject to its limitations, but it is not an equilibrium when those limitations are removed. Thus when we are concerned with the relation between the restricted optimum and the fuller optimum, it need not be confusing if we refer to the latter only as an 'equilibrium'. The practice of doing so is in fact well established; if it is understood in this way it does not need to cause trouble.[7]

[7] I do not think there is any inconsistency between what is said in this chapter and what I have said on similar matters in my *Causality in Economics* (1979), esp. pp. 39–46.

3
STATIC METHOD IN DYNAMIC THEORY

I have been insisting, in the preceding chapters, that static theory has a place, a place of its own, as something more than a preliminary to dynamics. There are problems, of applied economics, where a static approach is perfectly appropriate. But there are others for which it is not appropriate. For the study of such problems we need dynamic methods.

It took much time for this to be seen, or even to begin to be seen. It is not sufficient to think of what happened as a revolution, made in 1936 by Keynes. Keynes does indeed have a most important part in the story, but it is quite a complicated place. There can be no question that in his time there was a turning-point, and that it was Keynes who drew attention to it. But did the *General Theory* come at that turning-point, or before it, or after it, or (somehow) inside it? This is a question on which, we shall find, there is much to be said.

We are clearly obliged, in order to deal with it, to go back before Keynes. And we shall find that it is useful to go a long way back.

It is not at all true that the 'classical' economists of the eighteenth and nineteenth centuries were uninterested in dynamic problems: the causes of economic progress (as they called it) were one of their main concerns. And though in the post-classical period of 1870–1920 the interest was less, it was by no means wholly extinct. What is true (especially, we shall see, of Adam Smith and Ricardo) is that they had a very special approach to dynamic problems; their *method* of treating them was by the tools of static theory. I shall not refuse to reckon this as one of the 'Methods of Dynamic Economics'; for the phenomena to which it is applied are dynamic, though its method is static. We shall have to look at it very carefully, to see what it can do, and where it fails.

We can best approach the static method in terms of considerations which apply to all methods.

Any process of change can be exhibited, if we choose, as a sequence. The process is divided into steps, or stages, which can be taken separately and analysed separately; then, as best we can, we may fit them together. It is indeed not necessary to proceed in this manner. It is sometimes useful to work with continuous time. But it is probably wise to regard the analysis by stages as more fundamental. It is certainly my experience that it is the better way with which to begin. Distinctions which need to be made, and which come out clearly in period analysis, are not always so clear when we take time to be continuous. Besides, if one starts with stages, one can always proceed to a continuous statement by shrinking the duration of the stages; and it is not so easy to proceed the other way round. And we cannot wholly dispense with the discontinuous treatment, for business men think in time periods, and it is terms of time periods that they do their accounts.

In the discontinuous treatment we begin with the working of the model in a unit period (week, or month, or year); then we proceed to a sequence of such periods. There is of course a sense in which we do the same thing in statics; only in statics the periods are exactly alike, so one will serve for all. In dynamics the single periods (as we shall call them)[1] will not be alike, or not exactly alike; but they will still have some common features, so that much of the analysis can be made repetitive. Much of the work can be done on a *representative* single period: this single-period analysis is always a first step. But it is never the only step in a dynamic theory: some means of linkage between successive single periods must also be provided.

Some such layout as this is needed for every method of analysis of a dynamic problem, if it is taken sequentially. Thus what in the last chapter we called 'equilibrium at a point of time' becomes the equilibrium of the single period; what we called 'equilibrium over a period' becomes equilibrium over a sequence of single periods. The particular characteristic of the static method is to be identified within this general framework. It is simply this: that static theory is used as the single-period theory of the dynamic process. In each single period, the model is taken to be in static equilibrium. The process is reduced to a sequence of static equilibria.

Now it may well seem (and has obviously seemed to many people) that there is nothing very bad about this, that it is no worse than the things that have already been swallowed in static theory. Even in the purely static comparison of states we do not (as shown)[2] have to

---

[1] We need some special term for them; they must not be confused with the 'short period' of Marshall (see below, pp. 45–6).

[2] See above, p. 8.

believe that the economies under comparison are in fact unchanging; all that we do is to represent their average performance over time by that of a model economy which is unchanging at this average. Are we doing anything different here? It is certainly true that an actual economy will be changing all the time; however we divide its story up into sub-periods, they will be periods during which change continually occurs. Is it any more than a natural simplification to make the period uniform, and to concentrate change at the junctions? Are we doing any more than that when we take the single period to be in static equilibrium?

If we were doing no more, the procedure would indeed be harmless; uniformity of that sort must be supposed in any dynamic method that analyses change sequentially. The crucial characteristic of what we are calling the static method is different from that. It is (as it was expressed in the last chapter) that the equilibrium of time t could be taken to be determined by *current* parameters only: or, as we may put it now that we are using a sequential framework, that the equilibrium of the single period may be treated as *self-contained*. In a fully static theory this is a perfectly harmless assumption. Nothing has to be said, in statics, about the obvious point that production takes time, so that it must be oriented, not towards the present, but towards the future; for if present and future are identical we can substitute one for the other without making any difference. We can take a demand curve (for instance) which reflects current wants, and set against it a supply curve that refers to current production; for the same demand curve will still be 'there' when the process of production is completed; we do not have to bother about the fact that they refer to different *times*. But in dynamics these things do matter; it is of the essence of the dynamic problem that present and future are not identical.

Proper dynamic theory, even at its single-period stage, must take account of the fact that many activities that go on within the period are oriented outside the period; so that what goes on, even within the period, is not only a matter of tastes and resources, but also of plans and expectations. In statics there is no planning: mere repetition of what has been done before does not need to be planned. It is accordingly possible, in static theory, to treat the single period as a closed system, the working of which can be examined without reference to anything that goes on outside it (in the temporal sense). But this is not possible in dynamics. Even at the single-period stage the links which relate the single period to the rest of the dynamic process cannot be neglected.

————————

If the single period is treated as being in static equilibrium, the new investment that is undertaken in that period is not significantly distinguished from the rest of production; the relative values of the new investment goods are determined, in static manner, by supply and demand conditions, in terms of the tastes and resources of that single period.[3] The relative values of old capital goods (those inherited by this single period from its predecessor) are also determined as part of the general equilibrium of the single-period system; and it will usually be implied, as a condition of static equilibrium, that these should be consistent with the values of the new investment goods. But the value of a capital good, considered as a means of production, depends upon the return that is expected from it over its whole life. If this is reckoned as determinable from the conditions of the single period, the assumption has been allowed to creep in that the conditions of the single period are expected to remain unchanged in future periods. This assumption can only be avoided if we can stretch out the single period to cover so long a time that the useful lives of the capital goods, that are used in the period, fall altogether within it. But it will usually be impossible to do this by any stretching out, and it will always be true that by lengthening the single period we make it less fitted to play its part as an element in a dynamic process.

There is indeed just one case in which we can use this device effectively, and it so happens that it is a case that is of historical importance. Suppose that none of the capital goods that are used are seriously long-lasting; or (what comes to much the same thing) that the only capital that is used is circulating capital. And suppose that production has a regular cycle (such as the annual cycle of agriculture) so that the periods of utilization of the various capital goods fit together. Such an economy has a natural, largely self-contained, single period. When economists were dealing with a world in which production on this pattern was of dominating importance, they had a standing invitation to the use (even in their theory of economic progress) of static method.

As we shall see in the next chapter, it is their use of a model of this kind which goes a long way to explain the special characteristics of the 'growth models' of Adam Smith and Ricardo; each of them tried to push on beyond it, but with no more than moderate success. Later, when manufacturing industry had moved much further into the centre of the stage, the use of such a model became inevitably less appeal-

---

[3] A model that fits the above description rather exactly is the theory of capital of Walras.

ing. The processes of manufacture are lengthy processes, with no clear dates in which (as a whole) they start or finish. No confinement within a 'period' can ever capture them. Still, there seemed for many years to be no alternative to static method. So the most thorough-going theories of the production process as a whole which appeared in the later part of the century were completely static: one need do no more than to mention as examples the 'General Equilibrium' theories of Walras and Pareto, and the 'Austrian' capital theory of Böhm-Bawark. They made no attempt to deal with *dynamic* problems. Even in the monetary field, where dynamic issues are hardest to avoid (and where, as we shall see, the breakthrough was first to occur) there was at that stage a dominance of statics.

It was this static monetary theory which Keynes called 'classical'. That it was the dominant theory, for half a century or more before the time when he was writing is not to be denied. Its centre-piece was the Quantity Theory of Money. If monetary theory is to be static, all it can do is to make comparisons between static equilibria; that is just what the Quantity Theory does. The constancy of velocity, on which in some sense it must rely, in order to predict the effect on prices of changes in the Quantity of Money, cannot easily be defended except as an equilibrium condition. If one tries to follow through a process of adaption to a change in the Quantity of Money, taken to be exogen-ous, it will surely be found that at some stage in the process at least velocity must vary.[4] But if one is only interested in the comparison of equilibria, that does not matter.

It has always been found that on a closer examination of monetary problems these things do matter. How was it then that in the latter part of the nineteenth century it proved so easy for economists to avert their eyes from such examination? The answer, I think, must largely be found in the apparent stability of the monetary system in those days—the great days of the Gold Standard. Changes in most price-levels were then very slow, and it was natural to look for their causes in change in the supply of the precious metals. It cannot in-deed, even now, be firmly asserted that for that time that was wrong. But before that time, in the age of the Classical Economists proper, surely things were different. At the beginning of the century, before the Gold Standard was fully formed, prices had been much less

---

[4] I have worked this out for a simple example in my *Economic Perspectives*, pp. 50–60.

stable. Now it is the case that in that earlier period we do find deeper discussions, which in my sense are more dynamic. Monetary theory, then, was not always so static as it later became. The outstanding examples are Thornton's *Paper Credit* (1802) and the essay on 'Consumption and Production' (probably written about 1829) by J. S. Mill. But these in their day did not make much impression; it has been left to ours to rediscover their importance.[5] The 'classical' theory, in Keynes's sense, was buttressed by the apparent support of Smith and Ricardo. In their case it must have been their static method which made them 'classical'. How this was will emerge in the following chapter.

[5] See the paper on Thornton, and that on 'Monetary Theory and History' in my *Critical Essays* (1967); also the essay on Mill in the third volume of my Collected Essays, *Classics and Moderns* (1983).

4

PRIMITIVE GROWTH MODELS —
ADAM SMITH AND RICARDO

The greater part of what I have here to say about Adam Smith refers to one chapter in his book, that entitled 'Of the Accumulation of Capital, or of Productive and Unproductive Labour'.[1] There can be little doubt that Smith intended this chapter to be regarded as the centre-piece of his whole work. Earlier chapters lead up to it; many of those that follow are applications of it. And the principles that are laid down in this chapter—'Parsimony, and not industry, is the immediate cause of the increase of capital', 'every prodigal a public enemy and every frugal man a public benefactor'—have been distinguishing marks of 'classical' doctrine, from his day almost (if not quite) to ours.

Apart from its crystalization in such easy to be remembered epigrams, it is indeed not so easy to make out just what it is that Smith is saying. There are two difficulties which beset the modern reader. One is the fact that distinction between branches of economics, or kinds of economic argument, was still in its infancy. Though (as I shall show) he is in fact working with a much simplified theoretical model, he writes as if there was no gap between this and almost bare description. For the purposes of the present discussion I shall discard these realistic remarks, and look solely at the pure model.

Secondly, the pure model is consistently carried through on the assumption that the only form of capital (the only form that matters) is circulating capital. This assumption is nowadays so unfamiliar, at least to those who have been brought up in the Anglo-American tradition of economics, that the sectorization (for that is what it is) which Smith bases upon it looks quite esoteric. He is however doing just the same thing with his schema as we are accustomed to doing with ours.

We concentrate attention on fixed capital. Thus we define gross investment as being equal to net investment (the increment of the whole capital stock) *plus* replacement of the using-up of old fixed capital. There is no fixed capital in Smith's (formal) model; but he does have

[1] *Wealth of Nations*, Book II, ch. 3.

something which corresponds to gross investment. This is what it has to be in his terms: net investment *plus* replacement of the using-up of circulating capital. The labour which is engaged in this 'gross investment' he calls 'productive labour'.

Thus it is productive labour which plays the same part in his system as gross investment does in ours. It is unproductive labour which corresponds to our consumption sector (though it has of course a much narrower coverage). It is called unproductive because it plays no part in the replacement and new production of (circulating) capital. There is nothing left over from the work that it does. It 'perishes in the very instant of its performance' as he says.

These then are Smith's two sectors. But it is easier to understand what he does with them when one appreciates that his was not the first two-sector model. It had a predecessor, the model of Cantillon and the Physiocrats; this was certainly known to Smith. Their model could be expressed in terms of Smith's, by saying that the only productive labour which they recognized was agricultural. There were other differences, some of which are of much importance.[2] It is nevertheless quite useful, for an understanding of Smith, to think of him beginning with a model that sectorized in the manner of this predecessor; then generalizing it (or trying to generalize it) so as to take account of other forms of productive labour, in manufacturing, building, and otherwise.

I am fortified in my belief that there is such a model—Smith's Original Model I shall call it—which we can detect as standing behind Smith, since I shall be able to show that we also find it standing behind Ricardo.

The single-period, in this Original Model, is a natural period, the agricultural year. The initial capital comes from last year's harvest; it is, it actually is, a certain quantity of 'corn'. This is transformed, by the production of the year, into another, presumably larger, quantity of corn. That is done (there is no reason why this should not be admitted) in two ways: by natural reproduction, the use of corn for seed, and by employing labour in cultivation. It is not in fact of much importance to distinguish between these uses. For we can simply add the corn which the labourer sows to that which he consumes; the total is the amount of corn which is used up in employing him. He is himself, in terms of the model, simply a part of the process by which the

2 They are discussed in my paper 'The Social Accounting of Classical Models' (*Collected Essays* III, essay 2).

harvest of one year is transformed into that of the next. So the whole of the corn which he absorbs may just as well be reckoned into his 'wage'. This wage also, it will be noticed, is a quantity of corn.

If the wage, in this sense, is given, the number of labourers who can be employed will be determined by the size of the capital stock—which is therefore, in this model, a wage-fund. If there was no employment of unproductive labour, all the labour being employed in growing corn, the whole economy would reduce to a Productive Sector, and that would be just an apparatus for making corn out of corn. Consider the working of such an economy in period (year) t. Let X_{t-1} be last year's output of corn; let w be the given wage, also in terms of corn; the number of labourers employed will then equal X_{t-1}/w. If p is the productivity of labour (the amount of corn produced by one labourer), this year's output will be $p\,X_{t-1}/w$; so that

$$X_t = (p/w)\,X_{t-1}.$$

The growth rate of the economy, measured in terms of this *gross* output, accordingly equals $(p/w)-1$.

This is what happens when the whole of the corn output is used as a (direct or indirect) input into corn production—when nothing escapes outside. Ordinarily there will be a 'leak'. Some part of last year's harvest will be used for paying wages to non-corn producers (unproductive labourers); some may even be consumed directly by non-labourers.[3] The capital that is used in corn production in year t (K_t) will then not be the whole of the previous year's production, but only a part of it. Write $K_t = k\,X_{t-1}$ (with $k<1$). The number of labourers employed in corn production with then be K_t/w. So

$$X_t = (p/w)\,K_t = k\,(p/w)\,X_{t-1}.$$

The growth rate of the economy is thus no more than $k(p/w)-1$. Its growth is slowed down by its unproductive consumption.

This is evidently the message that Smith wanted to give; in the Original Model it is perfectly clear. But Smith was not content with this Original Model. His productive labour was not to be confined to agricultural. That creates two sorts of trouble. In the first place, capital (and output) cease to be homogeneous; secondly he loses the

[3] Adam Smith and his followers did not always draw attention to this possibility. 'But it makes better sense of the story to put it in, and the model can accommodate it without any inconvenience.

natural period of agriculture, which in the Original Model had made the single period self-contained.

The first of these losses is rather obvious: Smith certainly saw it, and (as we shall see) he thought he had found a way of dealing with it. I am not so sure that he did see the second, and it may well be that it is the more important.

In the Original Model the year is the accounting period. X_{t-1} is handed on at the beginning. X_t is carried forward at the end; they are just the opening stock and the closing stock of the year's accounts. All other items of the year, w, p, and k, are parameters of the year. Nothing, accordingly, is implied about constancy of these parameters between this year and its successor. So there is no need to interpret the model as a model of a steady state, in which these parameters remain constant over time. If, next year, the parameters were different, the growth would be different. There can surely be no doubt that this was the way in which Smith would have wanted his model to be understood.

In Smith's own model, the accounting period has become conventional; it can have nothing to do with the periods of production of the various goods. So the stock that is brought in at the beginning of the period can no longer be reckoned to consist entirely of finished goods.[4] It must largely consist of goods in process, goods which will have to have further work done on them before they can pass into consumption. If they are finished during the period, they will be available for consumption during the period; but they may not be finished until after the end of the period, so they will still be goods in process at the end. And of the productive labour that has been engaged during the period, some will be finishing the consumption goods of the period, but some will be making things which will go into the final capital stock. So the processes of production which appear during the period are no more than parts of processes which extend beyond the period, both before it and after it. They cannot be confined to the period, as they could be in the Original Model.

Now consider the bearing of this on the way in which Smith thought he could deal with the other problem, that of heterogeneity. If the more complex model is to be reduced into terms of the Original Model, some means must be found of reducing the opening stock, the

---

[4] So it is no longer possible to think (as some later economists, following the Original Model too closely, were inclined to think) of the initial capital as a 'Subsistence Fund' consisting of *previously accumulated* consumption goods.

closing stock, and the current output, to a common measure. The solution which Smith adopted was to value at cost. The initial capital would thus be reducible into terms of the labour that had been expended to produce it; this, in a circulating capital model, should be identifiable. But this labour is now not labour of the period; it is past labour. It is labour that *was* applied, before the beginning of the period. One cannot, without going outside the period, get a cost value for the initial capital.

But now consider the parallel problem of valuing output. This also, he clearly holds, should be valued at cost. But if, in the Original Model, the corn output had been valued at its labour cost alone, should we not have to have reckoned it as wL instead of pL? There would then have been no profit, or surplus, from which the employment of unproductive labour, or accumulation of capital, could have been provided. So, if the structure of the Original Model is to be carried over, the cost at which output is valued must include an allowance for profit. That, beyond doubt, was seen by Smith. Though his value theory is often called a labour theory (and though it is true that he takes labour to be the standard in terms of which values are reckoned) he must insist that his costs are to be taken inclusive of profit, so that p and w can be kept distinct.[5]

But what profit? There was no occasion, in the Original Model, for establishing a common rate of profit. There might be different rates on different 'farms'; the rate of profit, as calculated in that model, need be no more than an average. Here that will not do. If each of the goods that are included in output has its own rate of profit, no coherent measure of value for the different products has yet been found. Cost will have given no help in comparing the quantities of the different products with one another. So there must in some sense be a common rate of profit. But why should such a common rate of profit exist?

It would seem to be necessary, for it to exist, that the system, in the period, should be in *equilibrium*. Resources (of capital and labour) must be transferable from one use to another; and they must have been transferred, from less profitable to more profitable uses, until the common rate of profit has been established. Though an actual economy, in an actual period, will not be in equilibrium, it must be replaced, for purposes of analysis, by a model which is.[6]

[5] This is what he means by his distinction between 'labour embodied' and 'labour commanded' which has, very naturally, caused much mystification.

[6] Smith is quite clear about this. Consider his distinction between market and natural price. That is the point.

Further, this equilibrium must be quite far-going. For, as we have seen, we cannot value the initial capital of the period without going back to the labour of preceding periods; it now appears that we cannot value it, consistently with a cost measure of output, without attention to profit earned in preceding periods. And if there is to be full consistency between these two measures, we must in the valuations use the same rate of profit. So it is not only necessary that the model should be in equilibrium during the period: it must have been in equilibrium in the past as well.[7]

It should however be noticed that this long-run equilibrium—this very static long-run equilibrium which we have to attribute to Smith's model when we examine it closely—is an equilibrium of prices, or values, not necessarily of quantities. One can conceive of an economy where all production was conducted under constant returns to scale; there could then be changes from one set of quantities produced to another, without prices (equilibrium prices) changing. If relative prices do not change, when the growth rate of the economy changes, the composition of capital would change and the composition of output would change; yet we should still be entitled to treat their totals as measurable entities, measured in terms of any one of their constituents, so the way would be clear for the application of the Original Model. Growth would be greater the larger the part of output that was invested or re-invested; the less, that is, that was diverted from the employment of unproductive labour.

That is one way in which one can make sense of Smith; but it cannot, rather obviously, convey the whole of his meaning; for he insists, in his chapters on division of labour at the very beginning of his book, that he rejects the assumption of constant returns to scale. Nevertheless, in his value theory he finds it hard to escape it. The Original Model, or something like it, is always at the back of his mind, and to follow the pattern of the Original Model a 'constant cost' assumption is needed.

It is because he is following that pattern that he is, in Keynes's sense, so 'classical'. There is no problem, in the Original Model, about the transmission of saving into investment, for in that model there is no money. Indeed, there is hardly any exchange. One would be quite entitled to think of the landowners (or capitalists) into whose possession the harvest comes just piling it up in their store-houses;

[7] The past, not the future: all valuation at cost is backward-looking.

then doling it out to those whom they employ, productively or un-productively. Those employed are thus paid for their services, and that closes the matter as far as they are concerned. If they are paid in money, then spend the money on their 'corn' consumption, the money just comes back where it was without making any difference. There does not seem to be any harm in leaving it out.

Smith's own model, no longer so purely agricultural, must of course be money-using. It depends on exchanges, even (when one thinks it out) on both direct and indirect exchanges, and on borrowing and lending. It is inconceivable that such an exchange economy could exist without something in the nature of money. But in long-term equilibrium that money would not matter. Everything could be fixed up in advance without any money changing hands. Money is just a 'veil'—in equilibrium!

There is this reliance on equilibrium in Smith; much of what he says cannot be understood unless we stress it. But how does he recon-cile it with his other emphasis, on increasing returns? One can see how he thought he had found some sort of reconciliation.

Take the Original Model and suppose it to be in a steady state: p, k, and w are all of them constant from year to year; so, with capital being accumulated, the employment of labour must go on expanding. Where is this additional labour to come from? There are plenty of passages which make it clear that Smith had asked himself that ques-tion, or something which would correspond. He definitely holds that accumulation will raise wages, presumably because it creates a short-age of labour.[8] But the model seems to show that that will reduce the rate of profit, and so impede the accumulation. I do not think that Smith could, or would, have rejected this conclusion. If he does not stress it, this is because he holds that it would be offset by another, which he has been holding in reserve. It is not only w that would be higher in a progressive economy than in a stationary one, but also p—because of the division of labour. Increasing returns would come to the rescue!

But that is the point at which we have to turn to Ricardo.

———

For this was where Ricardo took off. Smith, it appeared, had granted the possibility that growth might be impeded by labour scarcity; but might it not be that there were other scarcities which could have a

---

[8] 'It is not the actual greatness of national wealth, but its continual increase, which occasions a rise in the wages of labour' (Oxford edn. 1976, p. 87).

similar effect? Ricardo was writing after Malthus,[9] and after it had
been demonstrated by the Napoleonic blockade that a country such as
Britain had great difficulty, in the circumstances of his time, in
feeding itself from its own resources; so it was very natural that the
inpediment to which he directed his attention was shortage of land.
The first way in which he will have wanted to modify the Smith model
was by the introduction of diminishing returns in agriculture.

We have the advantage of having two versions of the resulting
model. The first, which is given in the *Essay*[10] of 1815, carries on
directly from Smith; it is evidently a first sketch of what was to be
elaborated in the *Principles*, the first edition of which appeared two
years later. The kernel of the matter is in the *Essay*; it is easier to
understand the relevant sections of the *Principles* if we take the *Essay*
first.

There are simplifications in the *Essay* version which were later
removed. First, since his objective is to show the effects of a land constraint even if there is no shortage of labour, he assumes that there is
no shortage of labour so that expansion can continue at a real wage
which is fixed. (This has caused much trouble to later commentators;
it does *not* mean that the wage is fixed at a subsistence level.[11])
Secondly, again to sharpen the issue, he assumes that labour consumes no other product than that of agriculture, namely 'corn'.

The passage from the *Essay* version to that of the *Principles* consists
in the removal of these simplifications. But before we come to that let
us notice what powerful simplifications they are. Their first effect is
that they enable Ricardo to take his agricultural sector by itself. What
goes on in the rest of the economy does not affect what goes on in
agriculture. Then, beyond that, he can (here in agriculture) go back
to the Original Smithian Model, with its self-contained single-period,
the agricultural year. Capital, as in the Original Model, is circulating
capital, the corn output of the preceding year. He can concentrate
attention on what happens in agriculture in that self-contained
period.

The model that is constructed on this basis, in the *Essay*, is exhibited
by Ricardo in the form of an arithmetical table, a quite formidable
table, which it is not too easy to follow. It substance can however be
expressed in a more modern manner, in the form of a diagram (Fig. 1).

---

9 *Essay on Population* (1798 and 1802).

10 *Essay on the Influence of a Low Price of Corn on the Profits of Stock* (1815).

11 I owe this point to Samuel Hollander. See the paper which I wrote jointly with
him, 'Ricardo and the Moderns', which is reprinted in *Collected Essays* III.

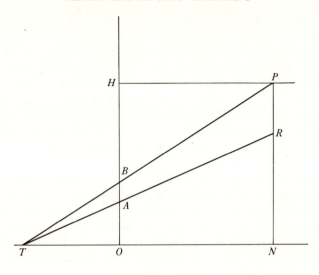

Fig. 1

Output (gross output) of corn is measured on the horizontal axis. On the vertical I measure the capital–gross output ratio. (Since both capital and output are measured in terms of corn, this, beyond any question, is a pure number.) The length OH is unity; so that the rectangle $OHPN$ represents the same quantity of corn, considered as capital (or input) as is measured by the length ON (when it is considered as output). Corresponding to the output ON, RN is the *marginal* capital–(gross) output ratio; that is to say, it is the quantity of corn that has to be used as input in order to produce an additional unit of corn output, when an output ON is already to be produced. The amount of land being fixed, diminishing returns can be expressed by making RN an increasing function of ON; thus we get the marginal 'curve' AR. As will be seen by checking through Ricardo's arithmetic, he takes this 'curve' to be a straight line—for no sufficient reason (this is of course a trick that is very liable to happen with arithmetical examples). I will follow him here in taking it to be a straight line.

At the margin, one unit of output ($PN = OH$ = one) requires RN of capital to produce it. Thus PR is the fraction of the marginal unit of output which is left as profit. The rate of profit on capital (at the margin) is thus equal to PR/RN. Now (says Ricardo), competition will keep the same rate of profit on capital being earned throughout the whole system; this will apply to intramarginal units in agriculture, as one case of its general application. We may show this if we produce RA backwards to meet the horizontal axis at T; and then join TP, cutting the vertical axis at B. For BA/AO is then equal to PR/RN; the same rate of profit is shown to be earned all along the 'curve'. Total profit is then represented by the trapezium $BARP$. If we now take the rectangle $OHPN$ to represent total output (as is clearly permissible), we at once see it falling into three parts: (1) $OARN$, which is replacement of capital, (2) $BARP$, which is profit, and (3) HBP, which is rent.

When the model is put into this form it looks easy to 'work' it. If the expansion of employment makes it necessary to expand agricultural output, population will 'press upon the means of subsistence'. N will therefore move to the right. But the AR curve is unaffected and T is therefore unaffected; the line TP must therefore swing downwards, for P must move to the right along the horizontal HP. The rate of profit must therefore fall, while rent rises.

Improvements in agriculture, diminishing the capital–output ratio, will cause the AR 'curve' to shift downwards, thus raising the rate of profit.[12] Importation from abroad, diminishing the output that has to be raised from domestic agriculture, will raise the rate of profit, since it will enable the TP line to swing to the left. And so on. These were the practical points which Ricardo wanted to demonstrate, but he could hardly hope that he had demonstrated them sufficiently by such a simplified model.

So he had to set to work to remove his simplifications. I do not believe that the first of them, the fixed real wage, gave Ricardo himself much trouble.[13] In spite of what he had learned from Malthus, it would be enough for him, on that side, to follow Smith. He would not want to say that the wage, all the time, would be at a subsistence level: all he needed to say was that the wage must be above some sort of a subsistence level if the supply of labour was to be expanding. But he would also say that the rate of profit must be above some minimum if the supply of capital was to be expanding. And it already followed from the *Essay* model that the higher the real wage the lower would be the rate of profit. Thus, although at a particular stage in the expan-

[12] There is of course no reason (as is at once apparent when the matter is looked at diagrammatically) why the curve should shift downwards uniformly (see Cannan, *Theories of Production and Distribution*, p. 323 ff.).

[13] Though it has caused much trouble to later commentators.

sion, when that was looked at by itself, the wage could be taken arbitrarily, it must lie within limits if both capital and labour were to be
expanding. And if, within these limits, the wage were too high and
profit therefore too low, there would *later* be not enough capital to
employ the increase in the labour supply (which had been generated)
at an unchanged rate of wages; while if the wage were too low, the
reverse would happen. There should thus be a level of wages, within
those limits, which could at least for a while be maintained. But since,
at an unchanged level of wages, the rate of profit must fall in the
course of expansion (as had already been shown in the *Essay*) a point
must be reached when both profits and wages have been reduced to
their minimum, so expansion stops—the stationary state.[14]

The other assumption, of labour consuming nothing but corn,
caused Ricardo much more trouble. For when that was gone it would
no longer be open to him to treat his agricultural sector by itself. He
did face that difficulty, but before we see how he did it, it is useful to
ask a preliminary question: what, in the model of the *Essay*, is supposed
to be happening in the rest of the economy, outside agriculture? We
are here to look at no more than a particular single-period, so the rate
of wages (here corn-wages) can be taken to be, within the limits, arbitrary.

If all of the 'outside' labour were unproductive labour, in the sense
of Smith, there would be no problem. Competition would keep the
wage of outside labour in line with the wage of agricultural labour;
since the latter is expressed in terms of corn, the outside wage must be
similarly expressed. The (equilibrium) price of each outside product
(here service) would be equal to the earnings of the labour required to
produce it. So these prices also would be determined in terms of corn.

Ricardo, however, preferred to assume that the outside labour is
productive labour, though that was bound to involve him in the
troubles about periods, which (as we have been seeing) were already
vexing in Smith. He began by cutting through them. Suppose that
outside production has a time-structure that is similar to that of agriculture; all products, like agricultural products, take a 'year' to produce. The self-containedness of the single-period can then be retained.
Uniformity of the rate of profit within the system will then ensure that
the prices of all products are *proportional* to the labour embodied (it being

---

[14] This can be set out formally in a diagram, as was done in the paper 'Ricardo and
the Moderns' which I wrote with Hollander (*Collected Essays* III, essay 4), and again in
Casuality in Economics p. 53. But Ricardo did not need to be so formal.

understood that in the case of corn, it is the labour required at the margin which must be taken). This is in fact the form of a Labour Theory of Value to which Ricardo does sometimes appear to commit himself (as in parts of the first chapter of *Principles*, 'On Value'); though it is perfectly clear that he did not hold to it more than provisionally.

If that is granted, the model of the *Essay* is easily completed. It is shown, as in Fig. 1 above, that the rate of profit in agriculture, being a rate expressed in terms of corn, is determined at the agricultural margin. The same rate of profit (still in terms of corn) must apply in outside production also. Outside wages are fixed in terms of corn; so it is the prices, in terms of corn, of the outside products which are determined, in equilibrium, by uniformity of the profit rate. Corn, throughout the model, is kept as the standard of value.

It was this characteristic of the *Essay* model which had to go, once it was admitted that the 'wage-good' contained other ingredients than corn; contained (that is) some of the outside products also. He had to look about for an alternative standard. A modern economist would seek to replace the corn by a composite wage-good, a 'basket of commodities'; but that did not occur to Ricardo.[15] He wanted to find a *particular* standard.

So long as he could hold to his 'Labour Theory of Value' assumption, of uniformity in the time-structure between the different branches of production, the solution seemed obvious. For the values of different products would then be changed in just the same way whatever changes in wages or profits occurred; so the relative values of the outside products would be unvaried. Any one of those products could then be taken as standard. It is fairly clear that at one stage of his thinking this is just what Ricardo did. For what results is the *Simple* form of the *Principles* model, a form which Ricardo was often content to use, when not specially concerned with further refinements.

Whichever of the outside commodities we take as standard, the (equilibrium) prices of the others, in terms of that standard, can thus be taken to be fixed. If the wage also is fixed, in terms of that standard, the rate of profit, again in terms of that standard, will be fixed.[16] The same rate of profit must rule in corn production, but while the labour costs of the outside commodities (Ricardo supposes) are inde-

---

[15] There were no index-numbers, it should be remembered, while he was living.

[16] $p_i = w a_i (1 + r)$, for each of the outside commodities, including the standard commodity (s). But $p_s = 1$. So $p_i = (p_i/p_s) = (a_i/a_s)$; that is Ricardo's 'labour theory'. Also, since $1 = w a_s (1 + r)$, if w is given, r is determined.

pendent of output, that of corn rises, at the margin, as output increases. So the price of corn, in terms of the standard, must rise as output increases.[17]

What is consumed by labour is largely, but not only, corn. So a rise in the price of corn, with a constant wage in terms of the standard, must reduce real wages, considering consumption as a whole. Thus if the wage remains unchanged, and the rate of profit therefore unchanged (both in terms of the standard), the real wage of labour must fall, in the course of expansion. So there must either be a fall in real wages, or a fall in the rate of profit, or a fall in both. But a fall in real wages, bringing the real wage nearer to the subsistence minimum, will check the increase in the supply of labour; while a fall in the profit rate will similarly check the accumulation of capital. Either way, therefore, the expansion of the economy will be retarded; which is in effect what Ricardo says.

That seems quite clear, in what I may call the Simple Model of the *Principles*; but it did not satisfy Ricardo. He wanted to go on further. He would drop the assumption that the outside commodities have the same production period as agriculture, and he would allow them to have different production periods among themselves. He must therefore allow that a change in the rate of profit would change the relative values of the different outside commodities.

This need not, in itself, have greatly changed the theory. Any one of the outside commodities could still have been taken as standard, and the argument could be pursued very much as before.[18] I shall, however, not follow him in that line of thought.

[17] In corn production, $p_c = wa_c\,(1 + r)$; but a_c is an increasing function of output.

[18] This can be seen by going to an extreme. Suppose that it is a pure service (of unproductive labour) that is taken as standard. Then, from the equilibrium of production of this standard, we have $1 = wa_s$; so w is a constant. We would then be unable to enquire into the working of the system at different w; so it is r that must be taken as independent variable. A rise in r will raise the costs of all the products of productive labour; so any average of the prices of products must be an increasing function of r: the 'real wage' must accordingly be a diminishing function of r. There will be some value of r which will reduce that real wage to subsistence; that sets a maximum to the r which is consistent with expansion of the labour force. It is obvious that this maximum will fall when a_c rises; a good deal more obvious than it is if one works with any other standard.

The trouble with this approach is that it is hard to imagine the capitalists–savers and the employers of labour doing their calculations in terms of such a standard; this is probably the reason why it did not appeal to Ricardo. His hope that he had found a solution by working in terms of a 'money' (presumably gold) which had a medium capital-intensity in production—so that some of the other commodities would rise in price and some fall, when r varied—is irrelevant to the present discussion. So I shall leave it on one side.

It is of much more importance, in the present context, to emphasize that the abandonment of the uniformity of periods of production, between corn and the various sorts of outside commodities, completely destroys the self-containedness of the single period, which in his Simple Model could still be retained. Ricardo himself does not appear to have noticed that he had involved himself at this point in the difficulty about equilibrium which we have seen to have been already implied in Smith. Equilibrium cannot now be confined to a single-period, such as the annual period of agriculture: his system must have been in static equilibrium much longer than that. I showed that there was in Smith a basic inconsistency, between the static equilibrium which he needed for one side of his argument and the increasing returns which he needed on the other. There is the same inconsistency in Ricardo, between his static equilibrium and his diminishing returns.[19]

I am not suggesting that Ricardo himself was aware of this inconsistency. I do not believe that he had identified the nature of the static method which he was using: how could he have done so while there was so little else with which it could be compared? Nor, even if he had done so, would he have felt himself to be committed to it: there is evidence to the contrary. There are parts of his work where he reaches out beyond it. Already, in the first edition of his *Principles*, there is a chapter on 'Sudden Changes in the Channels of Trade'; and to the third there was added the chapter 'On Machinery'. In each of these he is pushing on to the consideration of questions that need more than statics. But it is only in our day that attention has been given to these chapters.[20] It was the static part of Ricardo's theory which survived in the work of his successors, up to, and after, the end of the nineteenth century.

What could be done with the static method was done; but when it came to capital theory (self-containedness being no longer hoped for) all that could be done was the analysis of a stationary state, in which

---

[19] This, I think, was first observed by Carlo Casarosa, in his paper on 'The Ricardian System' (Oxford Economic Papers, March 1978). His attempted solution, by supposing the diminishing returns to operate in steps—so that a static equilibrium can be established at each step before the next is upon it—does not seem to me to be consistent with what Ricardo says (see the discussion in my *Causality*, p. 54). I find it more illuminating to recognize that the static equilibrium and the diminishing returns do not fit.

[20] I shall come back to that 'Machinery' chapter in Chapter 14 below.

data do not change, and in which (therefore) there is no accumulation of capital.

So the more precise capital theory became, the more static it became; the study of equilibrium conditions only resulted in the study of stationary conditions. But it was many years before anyone saw what was happening. Marshall saw it:

> A theoretically perfect long period . . . will be found to involve the supposition of a stationary state of industry, in which the requirements of a future age can be anticipated an indefinite time beforehand. Some such assumption is indeed unconsciously implied in many popular renderings of Ricardo's theory of value, if not in his own versions of it; and it is to this cause more than to any other that we must attribute that simplicity and sharpness of outline, from which the economic doctrines in fashion in the first half of this century derived some of their seductive charm, as well as most of whatever tendency they may have to lead to false practical conclusions.[21]

Wicksell saw it; it is marked in the very structure of his book. After concluding his Part II (in the first volume of his *Lectures*) in which he has set out his capital theory (his *stationary* capital theory), he passes to a third part (on accumulation) which is to be more 'dynamic'. But the third part is a mere fragment; though Wicksell saw the need for a more dynamic method, he did not go on to develop it himself. His successors did; but before we proceed to consider their contribution, we must examine how Marshall reacted to what he had seen.

[21] Marshall, *Principles*, 8th (or Variorum) edition, p. 379, note 1. It is interesting to find, from Guillebaud's collation, that the second sentence of the above quotation read originally:

'Some such assumption is really contained in many popular renderings of Ricardo's doctrines, which give them a sharpness of outline that he had never intended.'

The change was made in the second edition (1891). On reflection, it will be noticed, Marshall did not feel that he could throw the whole of the responsibility on to Ricardo's followers. And surely, in these second thoughts, Marshall was right.

5

THE METHOD OF MARSHALL

Marshall, it has just been shown, perceived the main issue with perfect clarity. He knew that static method (hitherto the only method of economic theory) led, when carried right through, to the stationary state, and no further. (The possible extension to a regularly progressive economy did indeed occur to him,[1] but he did not follow it up.) The theory of a stationary state seemed to him to be of little interest; if it was worth while to elaborate it at all, that was chiefly in order that it should not be mistaken for something else. What then was to be done?

There was, he thought, no alternative to statics. If a complete static theory led nowhere, we must make do with an incomplete static theory. We must lock up our difficulties in 'the pound of *ceteris paribus*'.

That, in short, is the method of Marshall. There is no question that it is a powerful method; for many problems of economics it is as good a method as we are likely to get. It is not at all a dynamic method; it is a resuscitation of statics. It was a special method which would only work in special cases (by Marshall's time, it is true, they were much more important cases). It would only work so long as the things that had been put into the 'pound' would stay there.

It may be observed that this same method was used by Marshall in at least two different ways.

The first was to fix attention (at least by preference) not upon the whole economy but on a sector (it had better be a rather small sector) of it: the partial equilibrium of the single 'industry'. In this, as in many other instances (it seems plausible to maintain), he got a hint from Ricardo. So long as Ricardo had stuck to his agricultural sector, his static method had served him well: it was when he tried to go beyond it that he got into trouble. Marshall would adopt the same device. Well aware that full static equilibrium meant stationariness, and believing that complete stationariness meant sterility, he would

[1] *Principles*, 8th edition, p. 368.

seek a way out by concentrating upon the 'industry'. It would not be so uninteresting to inquire into the conditions which would keep the single industry in full equilibrium. It would not then be necessary to postulate a complete cessation of change; it would be enough if the technique of the industry was not (autonomously) changing, if the terms on which the factors of production could be acquired were not changing, and if the demand curve for the product of the industry were to remain fixed. These, in particular cases, would not be such unrealistic assumptions; besides, as Marshall never tired of emphasizing, the theory made no claim to be a *precise* theory—it would be quite sufficient if the assumptions just listed were very approximately true.

That is one way in which Marshall applied his method; the other is the device (as I think it is proper to call it) of the *short* and of the *long period*. These, it will perhaps be as well to re-emphasize, have nothing to do with the sense of 'period' as it appears in truly dynamic economics (or as we have used it in our discussion of Smith). They are technical terms of Marshallian economics; when they are used by a modern economist one should look for a Marshallian reference. The 'long-period equilibrium' of the industry is the full equilibrium of the industry, with nothing more 'impounded' than the things that were listed in the previous paragraph. In the 'short period' impounding has been taken one stage further.

The supply of specialized skill and ability, of suitable machinery and other material capital, and of the appropriate organization has not time to be fully adapted to demand; but the producers have to adjust their supply to the demand as best they can with the appliances already at their disposal.[2]

It will be important to look closely at this concept and to appreciate, as exactly as we can, the use (as we shall see, the very peculiar use) that Marshall made of it.

———————

There is of course no question that (when 'period' is taken in its natural, non-technical, sense) there is always more flexibility in production when a long period is allowed for adjustment. If we take our stand at a particular historical date and look forward, the things that are to be produced in the following month have already been largely determined by past decisions; no change in demand can make much impression upon them. If we lengthen the 'short period' to three

———————

2 Marshall, p. 376.

months, there is more flexibility. That is true; but it was much more than that that Marshall was saying.

The crucial assumption, which is the distinguishing mark of Marshall's method, is that the *industry* in the *short period* can be treated as if it were in static equilibrium. (Marshall, it should be noted, only made this assumption with respect to the partial equilibrium of the industry;[3] its extension to the whole of a closed economy does not come until Keynes, and when it does so it raises other questions.[4]) In the *short period*, then, the fixed equipment of the industry being given (it will be sufficient to confine ourselves to the industry), the model has become similar to the agricultural sector of Ricardo. The fixed capital has become like land, 'original' and 'indestructible' *within the period*. Within the period it earns a rent, *quasi-rent* as Marshall called it.

It will be helpful to look at this procedure in the light of our previous discussion. Marshall, we may say, was treating his *short period* as a single period, in the manner of Smith or Ricardo, and invoking the constancy (or approximate constancy) of the fixed capital stock of the industry as a justification for treating the single period as self-contained. As he would doubtless have admitted, this could give him no means by which he could string his single periods together, so as to combine them into a dynamic process. In a dynamic economy there will be changes in the capital stock in any time period, however 'short'; these changes are an essential part of the linkage that ties one single period to another. Marshall's method just leaves them out.

Even apart from that, is he justified in taking his *short period* to be self-contained? It is implied by the self-containedness (and this agrees with Marshall's usage) that the output of the industry, in the *short period*, is solely determined by (1) the state of demand in that period, (2) the fixed capital stock, and (3) the terms in which inputs, such as those of labour and of materials, can be acquired *within the period*. Now, it is not to be denied that these things will often be the important things; whenever they are the important things, the *short-period equilibrium* will be a fair approximation to a complete analysis; and that is all that Marshall (no doubt) would have claimed it to be. There is, however, no reason in general why they should be the only important things; whenever they are not, the inadequacy of the Marshall method will be at once apparent.

---

[3] I dare say that there are passages where he allowed himself to slip into a wider application; but I am sure that the above statement is broadly true.

[4] See Chapter 6, below.

One of the things which Marshall left out (which he had to leave out) was what Keynes was later to call *user cost*. If the rate of usage of the fixed capital has any effect (in either direction) upon the measures which will have to be taken for its future replacement, there is an element in the cost of production which will not fit into the static scheme. For the valuation of this usage depends on what is to happen—what is expected to happen—outside the *short period*. It cannot be considered at all without introducing into the model something that is more *dynamic*.

Another is stocks (or inventories). It cannot be assumed that the values set, within the short period, upon materials absorbed are determined entirely within the period. That would only be so in an economy where there was no carry-over, so that everything that was absorbed within the period was produced within the period. This is almost nonsense, in view of the time taken in production (of which Marshall made so much). The values that are set upon materials, so long as they are durable enough to be stockable, must depend upon expectations.

The common element in these two omissions may be put in a more general way. Whenever there is a possibility of *substitution over time* (as I called it in *Value and Capital*[5]) the self-containedness of the *short period* will break down.

Nothing has so far been said, in this discussion of Marshall's *short period*, about the particular aspect of his analysis which has figured, more than any other, in later controversy: the question of the market form (competitive or monopolistic, more or less competitive or monopolistic) that is being assumed. I do not think that it has been necessary to say anything about that up to now: the status of the short-period equilibrium, form the points of view so far discussed, will be the same whatever is the market form. There is, however, another aspect from which a particular question of form turns out to be of major importance; at the point we have now reached, where we are at the threshold of more genuinely dynamic theory, we must give it the most serious attention.

What was Marshall's justification for treating his short-period model not merely as being self-contained, but also as being in equilibrium? How far, that is, can we expect that the performance of an industry (for we had better keep to an *industry*), over a month (say) of

[5] p. 208.

time, will be reasonably well represented by its short-period equilibrium? Even if substitution over time is neglected, so that it is accepted that *current* demands (and so on) are the only things that determine what firms will want to produce, why should we assume that what they want to produce is the same as what they sell? Equality between demand and supply, in the sense of amount bought and amount sold, is an identity which has nothing to do with the equilibrium assumption. Equality between amount sold and the amount which, in the given circumstances, sellers will want to sell is quite a different matter. Sense can be made of it over a long period; but when it is applied to a short period, it looks a very dubious assumption indeed.

Nevertheless, Marshall made it; and I am not suggesting that he did not know what he was doing.[6] There is a way in which his procedure can be justified, for his own purposes; but the justification does not extend to the use which has been made of his procedure by later economists. There is a distinction which it is most important to make.

In order to see how Marshall himself would have justified his procedure, we must turn to a part of his argument which has so far been left out. This is the theory of price determination in the 'ultra-short period': market equilibrium when the quantity to be sold is itself a part of the data, having been determined by decisions that, when the market opens, are already in the past. This is expressed, in Marshall's manner, in the form of an analysis of a 'corn market in a country town'. (It is rather a curious corn market, in that the corn is oddly assumed to be non-storable; for this reason it became common, in later Cambridge tradition, to replace 'corn' by 'fish'.) Buyers and sellers are supposed to come to the market without knowledge of the equilibrium price—the price that will equate supply to demand. Transactions may thus take place, initially, at arbitrary prices. But it is Marshall's contention that the final price, at which the last transactions will take place, will be approximately the same as the equilibrium price. Even though there are initial sales at 'false' prices, the final price will be much the same as that which, if it had been fixed at the start, would in fact have proved to be capable of being carried through.

It is by benefit of this principle that Marshall's 'corn market' is enabled to dispense with artificial arrangements, like Edgeworth's

---

[6] He might, admittedly, have explained himself more fully; he would have spared his successors a lot of worry if he had done so.

'recontract' or the 'crying of prices' of Walras. The purpose of these was to find a way by which early bargains could be undone if the prices at which they were made did not correspond with the equilibrium price. Marshall maintains that, even if they cannot be undone, it does not matter. For the effect of a bargain at a 'false' price is just to redistribute purchasing power from buyer to seller, or from seller to buyer, according as the 'false' price is too high or too low. The effect of that redistribution is an income effect; all that matters (from the point of view of price determination) is the shift which it produces in the demand curve for the 'corn'. If expenditure on 'corn' is only a small part of total expenditure, that shift is unlikely to be considerable. Therefore, in this 'ultra-short' period, the static determination of the price by equilibrium of demand and supply will give a fair approximation to what is likely to happen in practice.

It is unnecessary to go into any greater detail about the 'corn market';[7] I have not introduced it here for its own sake but for what follows on from it. Something very similar must have been supposed by Marshall to hold for the *short period* proper. (There can really be no doubt about that; otherwise why should he have bothered about the 'corn market'?) It is not output only, *it is also price* which is supposed to be determined by equilibrium of demand and supply, in the short period.

This is where the question of what is implied about market form becomes important. The distinction which I have in mind is not quite the same as the usual distinction between perfect and imperfect (or monopolistic) competition; but it is nearly the same—the one distinction very often corresponds to the other. There has been much discussion[8] about the precise character of the competition that is assumed by Marshall. It is now accepted that his model is not a strict perfect-competition model, like that of Walras. His firms experience internal as well as external economies; they hold back for fear of 'spoiling the market'. That is true, but it is also true that in the particular respect that concerns us here Marshall is on the perfect-competition side of the fence. His firms are not 'price-makers', as we have learned to think firms to be when they operate in an imperfect market. Prices are not set by firms and then altered if they turn out to be 'wrong'.

---

[7] I have myself discussed it in more detail elsewhere. See the Note to Ch. 9 of *Value and Capital* (pp. 127–9).

[8] Since the days of the 'Cost Controversy' (*Economic Journal*, 1926 and after).

They are more flexible than that; so they can be *determined* by demand and supply, by the bargaining of the market.

I suggest that this aspect of Marshall's model is nothing else but a straightforward reflection of actual conditions in England in the late nineteenth century: at the time, that is to say, when Marshall was writing. The standardized and branded goods, which are the typical consumers' goods of present-day economic organization, had not then appeared, though they were perhaps on the point of appearing.[9] The modern economist takes for granted that it is the manufacturer who fixes the price that the consumer is to pay; but in those days even manufactured goods usually passed along a chain of wholesalers and retailers, each of whom was likely to have some independent price-making opportunity. Nowadays, when demand increases, it is the manufacturer who decides whether (or when) to raise his price; when demand falls off whether (or when) to lower it. In Marshall's day it will quite usually have been the case that he had no such choice.

An increase in demand would not be allowed to remain unsatisfied or to run down stocks unduly. Price would rise, not because of any action by the manufacturer, nor indeed by the ultimate consumer (who, then as now, would normally be a passive party); the initiative would come from the wholesaler or shopkeeper, who would offer higher prices in order to get the goods which, even at the higher price, he could resell at a profit. Similarly, when demand fell it would be the wholesaler who would offer a lower price. The manufacturer would have to accept that price, if he could get no better, or else he must refuse the business for fear of 'spoiling the market' (as Marshall says).

This, I believe, is the kind of market from that Marshall was envisaging. It will be noticed that it does not much resemble the (Walrasian) model of *perfect competition*. It is consistent with a good deal of ignorance, not only on the part of the ultimate consumer but also on the part of the manufacturers, and even (but to a lesser degree) on the part of the intermediary traders themselves. Plenty of trading will then go on at 'false' prices. It will nevertheless be true that in the *short period* (substitution over time being neglected) price is determined, at least roughly, by 'equilibrium of demand and supply'. That is all that Marshall needs for the applicability of his particular sort of static method.   ————————

[9] For a detailed description of the transition, in one particular case, see C. Wilson, *History of Unilever*, vol. II, pp. 64 ff. (See also B. S. Yamey, 'Origins of Resale Price Maintenance', *Economic Journal*, 1952.) These, it will be noticed, were developments of the period between 1890 and 1914.

Marshall was indeed a great economist. If, in this chapter, attention has been mainly directed to some limitations of his analysis, I hope it has been done in a way which makes it clear how much he could do in the directions in which (naturally enough, at his date) he preferred to work. Our problems, however, are not his; we must not expect to be able to use his methods for purposes for which they were not designed.

One of the reasons why we need other methods (as we shall see more specifically dynamic methods) is that we are now more interested in macro-economic problems, from which (for reasons that have been explained) Marshall had, on the whole, to turn aside. But there is also another reason: that the market forms in which we are especially interested are different from that which he took as typical. It will nevertheless prove to be useful to have unearthed this point about market forms; for we shall need to have it before us when we are considering Dynamic Theory proper. It is desirable that Dynamic Economics (or that branch of it which is a part of Pure Economics)[10] should be able to deal with a variety of market forms. Marshall's form is thus still worthy of study, though we should study it in a way which makes it possible to study other forms too.

Though the method of Marshall can be regarded, as I have (on the whole) regarded it here, as a last stage in the evolution of static method, it gets very near to dynamics. It is the beginning of one of the transitions to dynamics, which we shall be following through in the chapters which follow.

[10] See above, p. 6 ff.

6

THE METHODS OF KEYNES

One has to talk about Keynes's methods, in the plural, since there are so many of them. It is not merely that there were changes of method between his three main books on money—the *Tract on Monetary Reform* of 1923, the *Treatise on Money* of 1930, and the *General Theory* of 1936. Even in the *General Theory* itself, the main method is a hybrid, a combination of two which it is useful to distinguish. And there are the beginnings of other methods also.

For during the years in which these books were written, his thought went on developing; and one can tell, from the slighter things that he was able to write between the *General Theory* and his death in 1946, that the *General Theory* itself was not the end of that development. We do not get it into focus if we look at it by itself.

———

From the theoretical point of view, the *Tract* is conventional. The Quantity Theory, he tells us himself, 'is fundamental' (p. 74). Great stress is laid on the variation of velocity (or of the willingness to hold money) between booms and slumps; deliberate variation in the quantity of money, to counteract those changes in velocity, is strongly recommended. Monetary policy should be directed towards stabilizing the price-level (there is no suggestion of there being more than one price-level) rather than towards stabilizing the rate of exchange. All this could be said, and in the *Tract* it is said, without going outside the bounds of static theory. It is just the *states* of boom and slump that are being (statically) compared.[1] And nothing at all in particular is said about wages.

———

When one turns to the *Treatise*, there is a great change. What is 'fundamental' is no longer the Quantity Theory, but those celebrated 'Fundamental Equations' which so perplexed his readers. I think I can show, by some changes in notation, how to make them,

———

[1] The section on forward exchanges, which to a modern reader is the most exciting part of the *Tract*, may be admitted to be in some ways a little more dynamic. But the interest-parity theorem, on which it depends, is a static theorem.

now, much more intelligible. I can also show how the change came about.

The clue, as so often with Keynes, is what was happening around him. Between the dates of the *Tract* and of the *Treatise* came the restoration of the Gold Standard in Britain, to which Keynes had responded by attacking it in his famous pamphlet, *The Economic Consequences of Mr. Churchill* (it was in Churchill's 1925 budget that the decision had been announced). It is here that we find the turning-point. For it is extremely significant that the main ground of his attack was not his general preference for price-stability over exchange-stability, as might have been expected from the author of the *Tract*. It was his conviction that the par which had been fixed was inconsistent with the level of money wages, which he held to be firmly established. (It may be remarked that it was very recently that it can have got so established. Money wages had moved a lot during the War and post-War; 'stickiness' can hardly have set in before 1922. It is not surprising that in the *Tract* Keynes had paid no attention to it.)

Rigidity of wages is central to the *Treatise* model. It is not necessary, for that model, to make wage-changes completely exogenous; it would be enough for their response to the state of the market to be very slow. There was nothing new about that, as an observation. We find it as far back as Hume's *Essay on Money* (1752). It is explicit in Henry Thornton (1802) who says, in so many words,[2] that 'the rate of wages is not so variable as the price of goods'. There is no reason to suppose that those nineteenth-century writers whom Keynes called 'classical' would have denied it, as a fact. They just regarded it as being of no importance, because they were solely concerned with comparative statics, where speeds of adjustment did not matter. For Keynes, already in 1925, they did matter.

Because of the inconsistency between wages and the exchanges, Britain was in what classical theory would have called a disequilibrium situation. But there was no classical theory of such situations. So Keynes set out to construct one. That is what, in the theoretical part of the *Treatise*, he is doing. He is looking for a general theory of what happens when prices and wages are out of line.

He begins with a closed system, leaving foreign relations for later discussion. Thus the only source of disequilibrium which it is open to him to introduce is an expansion (or contraction) of credit. What will

---

[2] p. 159 of the Hayek reprint of *Paper Credit*.

be its effect on prices, the prices of commodities, before wages have had time to move?

This concentration on prices is characteristic of the *Treatise* model; to us, who know what was to happen afterwards, it is bound to be startling. Effects on output, and on employment, which were later to move so much into the centre of the picture, are entirely disregarded. (Was this a relic of Quantity Theory problematics? Keynes was writing a book about money.) So his disequilibrium is solely one of prices (and profits). These are considered by themselves.[3]

The form which he gave to his answer, to the question thus posed, is clearly, so it seems to me, derived from Marshall. Being himself a product of that great school of economics, which Marshall had established at Cambridge, it was natural that he should look to Marshall for guidance. Marshall, as we saw,[4] was concerned with the response, in a single industry, to an increase in demand for the product of that industry; he had dealt with it by looking at an intervening stage, his short-period equilibrium (SPE I shall call it) where firms had to satisfy the increased demand, as best they could, with equipment, now inappropriate, which had been more or less appropriate to the previous state of demand. Not until a new, more appropriate, equipment had been got ready could the industry pass into long-period equilibrium (LPE). It was a construction of this type which Keynes took over.

What in the *Treatise* is called 'equilibrium' matches the LPE of Marshall. It is characteristic of each that prices are in line with costs, costs that are based on given wage-rates. Marshall could take the wage to be given, in the industry of which he was thinking, because it would be based on conditions outside that industry. Keynes's given wages do not have, or need, that justification: wages do not change in his (LPE) 'equilibrium' because there is nothing to make them move.

In LPE, in Keynes as in Marshall, profits are *normal*. The normal profit of entrepreneurs is defined by Keynes as 'that rate of remuneration which, if they were open to make new bargains with the factors

---

[3] There is a parallel assumption in Sraffa's *Production of Commodities by means of Commodities*, in which (we are distinctly told in the preface) 'no changes in output are being considered'. Though not published until many years later (1960), we learn from that same preface that a first draft had been given as a paper in Cambridge in 1928, just when Keynes was writing the *Treatise*. Keynes was studying inflation without attention to production; Sraffa distribution without attention to production. Was there any connection?

[4] pp. 44–5 above.

of production at the currently prevailing rates of earnings, would leave them with no incentive to increase or to decrease their scale of operations'[5]—a definition which, not surprisingly, was later to cause much trouble. Costs are taken to include these normal profits, so it is an LPE condition that prices should equal costs.

Keynes is using the same division into sectors, consumption and investment sectors, as persisted in the *General Theory* and with which he has made us so familiar. It is accordingly not difficult to restate his analysis in *General Theory* notation.

Since, in LPE, prices equal costs, we have, in LPE

$$Y^* = I^* + C^*$$

where I^* and C^* are the values of investment-good production *at LPE prices* and Y^* is total income. (The corresponding relation, $Y = I + C$, must indeed hold quite generally, so long as the components are suitably valued.[6])

The LPE is now disturbed by an expansion of credit, the direct effect which is a rise in the prices of investment goods. Outputs (it must continue to be emphasized) remain unchanged. Thus, when the value of investment goods production increases from I^* to I, the ratio (I/I^*) expresses the rise in *their* price-level. The difference, $I - I^*$, which I shall follow Keynes[7] in calling Q_2, is an 'excess over normal' profit.

What, in the meantime, has been happening in the consumption goods sector? So far, nothing. For there has been no change in income (Y), except for the excess profits which are being earned in the investment sector. If no part of those excess profits is spent on consumption goods, there is no reason why the prices of those goods should change. So we should simply have, for the social accounts of this first 'disequilibrium' position,

$$I = I^* + Q_2, \quad C = C^*, \quad Y = Y^* + Q_2, \quad Y - Y^* = I - I^*$$

It is when a part of the excess profits goes to increase the demand for consumption goods that things become more interesting. If there is this consumption backwash, there will be excess profits in the

---

[5] *Treatise*, vol. I, p. 125.

[6] This does not fit with *Treatise* terminology, but we are surely entitled to introduce a social accounting identity, even though Keynes, at the stage of the *Treatise*, preferred not to use it.

[7] I like to keep this part of his notation; for his choice of Q is so obviously an echo of the *quasi-rent* of Marshall.

consumption sector also, and the effects of these must be allowed for. The social accounts will then have to read

$$I = I^* + Q_2, \; C = C^* + Q_1, \; Y = Y^* + Q_1 + Q_2 = Y^* + Q$$

if (like Keynes) we write Q for the total of the excess profits.

All these equations are no more than definitional; Keynes however went on to postulate a 'behavioural' relation between the excess profits (Q) and the share of this Q which is spent on consumption goods. Let s be the fraction which is not so spent. Then $C - C^*$ (the increase in the value of consumption goods production) $= (1 - s) Q$. But this, as shown, $= Q_1$. Thus $Q_2 = s \, Q$. So

$$Q = Y - Y^* = (1/s) \, Q_2 \; = \; (1/s) \, (I - I^*).$$

If there had been no backwash, the increase in income would have been equal to the increase in the value of investment $(I - I^*)$. The result of the backwash is that a *multiplier* $(1/s)$ is applied to it.

I do not think it can be doubted that what has just been set out algebraically is the kernal of the Fundamental Equations of the *Treatise*. But what meaning can be given to it? The conclusion has been put together from social accounting identities, with the one additional condition that the fraction s is given (somehow) independently. If it had not been given independently, it could still have been deduced from the rest of the accounts, which are identities, and which must therefore 'always' hold. Whatever happens in the process of adjustment, there must be some value of s which could be calculated. Unless a value for it is given independently, nothing about the process of adjustment has been explained.

It would be possible to construct a sequential model in which the backwash occurred in steps, the increment in C (the value of consumption) depending on the excess profits (Q) that had occurred in the *week* before.[8] But this, it is clear, is not what Keynes does. His C and his Q, being taken from the same set of accounts, have to be contemporaneous. But that only makes sense if the model has already reached an *equilibrium*, in which the backwash is completed, so that what happens in the current week and in the week before need no longer be distinguished. The 'disequilibrium' to which the Fundamental Equations refer must itself be an equilibrium.

---

[8] That is of course what Kahn was to do, very soon after the publication of the *Treatise*. But Kahn was already working in terms of output and employment, so in that other respect he was looking forward to the *General Theory*.

I do not believe that Keynes, in 1930, would have resisted that conclusion; it would have been quite congenial to his way of thinking. He
would have been happy to have his 'disequilibrium' match the SPE of
Marshall. It is a restricted equilibrium, like Marshall's.[9] I shall take it
in what follows that there is this correspondence.

It is indeed much harder, in this construction of Keynes's, than it was
in Marshall's, to accept that the SPE could go on, even for a while,
without 'other things' being affected. Flexible prices (not only
investment-good prices, but also consumption-good prices) have had
to be changed, at the end of what, when considered sequentially, is
quite a complicated process, without either wages, or output and
employment, having varied. Wages are to be rigid, because there has
not been time for them to change; but may not the full adjustment of
the flexible prices take too long? And is it conceivable that the full
adjustment of the flexible prices could be carried right through
without having effects on output and employment?

These were obvious objections to the *Treatise* model. We have surely
to think of Keynes deciding, not long after the *Treatise* left his hands,
that the second at least could not be resisted.

So he had to abandon the *Treatise* simplification, the study of price-
changes without quantity-changes. Quantity-changes had to be
allowed for. He wanted to study them in the same way as the price-
changes had been studied; so the natural way to begin was to seek to
construct a model in which quantities changed with no effect on
prices. Price-effects, at the least, had to be pushed into the background.

The transformation which this wrought upon the theory was
drastic. It was not possible for the new theory to be just a 'dual' of the
old. The structure of the theory had got to be changed.

For the distinction between the two sorts of equilibrium, the SPE
and the LPE which the *Treatise* had taken over from Marshall, could no
longer be maintained. In the LPE of the *Treatise*, profits are normal,
in the sense (as was stated) that entrepreneurs get no incentive from
them to change their 'scale of operations'. In the new model, which
was to become the *General Theory* model, scale of operations having
become a variable, equilibrium in this sense can be reached at any
level of activity. (There must indeed be a limit beyond which expansion cannot proceed, so full employment makes its appearance.) That

[9] See above, p. 44–5.

equilibrium is consistent with unemployment is one of the things on which he was now to insist. But just what was he now to mean by *equilibrium*?

He must surely have begun by taking it that equilibrium, in the new model, was to be defined in the way it had been defined in the *Treatise*; a condition in which entrepreneurs have no incentive to change their scale of operations, and hence the amount of employment they offer. This is entirely consistent with what has just been said: that the system might get stuck with a high rate of unemployment. But while in the *Treatise* that equilibrium was LPE, to be used as a base with which the 'desequilibrium' SPE was to be compared, it was no longer possible to use it in that manner. For the new equilibrium was to be reached by a multiplier process (as we now know so well); just the same sort of process as that by which the SPE of the *Treatise* had been reached. Thus though (so far) it is defined in an LPE manner, it is used in the way that the *Treatise* had used its SPE. There is now just one sort of equilibrium; but it has some of the characteristics of each of the parents from which it has sprung. But how is one to be sure that these characteristics are compatible?

The *Treatise* equilibria were static equilibria, like the LPE and the SPE of Marshall. They were static equilibria, in the sense that they could remain unchanged, so long as the things which had been taken into account in determining them remained unchanged. Can the equilibrium of the *General Theory* be in that sense static? It is very tempting to think that it can be; and there can surely be little doubt that Keynes, very often, thought it was. (For again consider his insistence that equilibrium is consistent with unemployment. That would be of no importance unless the equilibrium were static.) There can be still less doubt that many of his followers have thought that it was. For once that is granted, the way is open to what has become the standard way of applying *General Theory* analysis; just the way in which static analysis has traditionally been applied—comparative statics.[10] If investment had been different, or the propensity to consume had been different, what would have been the effect on employment? Once we think we know the answers to such questions, we can proceed to use them in the way they have so much been used, to make

[10] In my first review of the *General Theory*, written very soon after it came into my hands, I said that its technique 'is conservative, more conservative than that of the *Treatise*' (*EJ* 1936, *Collected Essays* II, p. 99). I think that this is what I meant. The *Treatise* was at least attempting to be a bit more dynamic.

recommendations about policy, the 'Keynesian' recommendations that are so familiar. But if we reach them that way, without going further, they are not too secure.

For there is a quite obvious reason why the equilibrium of the *General Theory* cannot be static. Saving and investment are flows, which extend over a period. It is accepted that what happens during the period depends not only on investment and saving propensities, but also upon the stock of capital goods with which the period opens. Now if, during the period, net investment is not zero (and it is surely intended that the model should apply more generally than to that special case) the stock of capital goods, at the end of the period, cannot be the same as at the beginning. So it is impossible for the behaviour of the economy, in the next period, just to repeat. The *General Theory* model, in the period examined, cannot be in a static equilibrium.

Now it seems to me that Keynes and his followers, though they could not have refused to admit that this was so, would have refused to let it trouble them. For could not the same objection, they might have said, have been brought against the SPE of Marshall? And Marshall would have had a way out. He could have accepted that in his SPE, when output is being produced with an equipment that is inappropriate, a more appropriate equipment will be in the course of construction, or on the point of being constructed. In the next period it will be nearer completion. But if it has not yet come into use, it will not yet affect the equilibrium of the product market, in which Marshall is interested. That market can remain in a static SPE, until the time comes when the new equipment is ready. That is all that Marshall needs. The confinement of his analysis to the study of a particular market gives Marshall a defence. But how is that defence to be adapted to a macro-theory, such as that of Keynes?

It would have to be insisted that the Keynes equilibrium, like Marshall's, is a restricted equilibrium, but it would have to be restricted in another way. It would have to be restricted to the determination of employment, within the period that is under consideration, taking that period *by itself*. It could then be static in the restricted sense that employment, during the period, would not be changing. Other things that are implied in the model, such as the capital stock (which would be changing), are not considered. We just put them out of our minds.

Though such a defence can rarely have been offered explicitly, it is fully in accordance with the Marshallian pedigree which I have been tracing; and it is fully in accordance with the way the Keynes theory has so often been read. So long as the period is looked at *by itself*, all that matters about the investment, during the period, is the employment that it gives, and the income that it generates. It does not matter, accordingly, whether the form that it takes is wisely or unwisely chosen. It is only when one looks further forwards that it does matter. The Keynes theory, so interpreted, is inherently short-sighted.

So it is not dynamic. Like Marshall's, it is quasi-static. As long as the period is taken *by itself*, it cannot be treated as a stage in a process. So the model cannot be used as the 'single-period' theory of a dynamic analysis, to which a theory of continuation, into subsequent periods, is to be joined. For a theory of continuation, the things that are carried over, at the end of the period, must be of major importance.

But this is only one way in which the *General Theory* can be taken. There are others, which take one much further. Some of them will be explored in later chapters of this book.

_____

It would, however, be wrong to conclude this chapter without saying a word on that large part of the *General Theory* which is concerned with interest and money—the 'LM curve' of the familiar diagram. In this case also it is useful to go back to the *Treatise*, perhaps even more useful; for while the *Treatise* multiplier is eclipsed by the *General Theory* multiplier, there are in the *Treatise* the beginnings of a theory of liquidity which is wider than that of the *General Theory*. Liquidity preference, in the later work, is solely a matter of one particular choice—that between the holding of non-interest-bearing money and the holding of long-term government securities, the yield on which is taken to represent the long-term rate of interest. But it is at least hinted, in the *Treatise*, that liquidity is relative—that it enters into the choice between holding any sorts of assets.[11] When this concept is given its head, the theory is transformed.

I myself have made a number of attempts at sketching out that wider theory, but I shall not discuss them here. Earlier versions[12] were 'quasi-static' like Keynes's; but the later[13] have I think become

[11] See especially, vol. II, p. 67.

[12] The first is my 'Suggestion for simplifying the theory of money' (*Economica* 1935, reprinted in *Collected Essays* II). This was written at a time when I had some acquaintance with the *Treatise*, but had not yet seen the *General Theory*.

[13] The main stages were 'The Two Triads' (*Critical Essays* 1967); the second chapter in *Crisis in Keynesian Economics* (1974); and pp. 72–80 of *Economic Perspectives* (1977).

more dynamic. The connection between liquidity and speed of reaction is the theme to which I have finally come.[14]

I shall be alluding to these matters, now and then, in the following chapters.

[14] 'Sequential Causality—Lags and Reserves' in *Causality in Economics* (1979).

7

THE TEMPORARY EQUILIBRIUM
METHOD

The first of the (properly) dynamic methods which I shall be considering is that which was developed, very deliberately developed, by Erik Lindahl in 1929–30.[1] Thus it was worked out at just the same time as Keynes's *Treatise*; but it was (at least initially) quite independent of the *Treatise*, nor did Keynes know anything appreciable about it until after he had written the *General Theory*. So this is the right place to consider it. It will join on very readily to what has been said in earlier chapters of this book, especially in Chapter 3.

Lindahl was himself quite a bit of a methodologist; he was fond of reflecting on what he himself had been doing. He thus came to be perfectly conscious that it was a new dynamic method that he was devising. But that, of course, was after the event. The method would not have been devised because there was a methodologist's pigeonhole for it; it was devised because there was a need for it. The particular place where the need was felt—in Sweden, as in contemporary England—was in monetary economics.

The phase in monetary thinking to which I am referring is (as should be evident by the dates) antecedent to the World Depression. It was the collapse of the pre-1914 International Gold Standard, and the conviction (which gradually prevailed) that that old 'monetary constitution' could not be restored, which had made the whole character of the monetary system an open question, as it had not been before, at least since the days of Thornton and Ricardo. Money was being looked at in a new way; new questions were being asked, and (as Lindahl says) they were what we have called dynamic questions. The stability that was sought—the monetary stability, stability of one

---

[1] I do not read Swedish, so my knowledge of the writings to which I am referring is limited. I did however make friends with Lindahl as early as 1933, and the substance of his Penningspolitikensmedel (1930)—to appear in 1939 as the second part of his *Studies in the Theory of Money and Capital*—was available to me from about the former date. At about the same time I read Gunnar Myrdal's *Monetary Equilibrium* in German; the Swedish version of that had also appeared in 1930, the English, again, not until 1939.

variable (for example, the price level) when other related variables are changing—is itself a dynamic property. It slips through the fingers when we try to deal with it by static methods. It requires, in order that we should be able to treat it, some way of analysing a process.

Swedish economists, coming to monetary theory in the nineteen-twenties, had an advantage in beginning from Wicksell; for in the doctrine of 'Interest and Prices'[2] they had a key that would open many doors, and (for a while) it remained very nearly their private possession. Even afterwards, when Keynes[3] and Hayek[4] had made Wicksell world famous, it was an advantage to the Swedes that for them his work was not a novelty. They did not over-estimate it, as those to whom it was new were at first tempted to do. In strictness, all that Wicksell had done (in the monetary field as in others) was confined to the analysis of stationary equilibrium. Something like what he had found for that case must (fairly obviously) be true much more generally. But *exactly* what would be true in non-stationary conditions was a thing that Wicksell had left for his successors to discover.

In Wicksell's stationary state, relative prices remain constant over time; and there is a rate of interest (Wicksell's *natural rate*) which is determined as part of this system of relative prices. Being part of the 'real' price system, which is closed and complete, without mention of money, so long as the economy is stationary, the natural rate is strictly to be interpreted as a rate of exchange between 'wine' now and 'wine' a 'year' hence; or, since relative prices are unchanging, between any good now and the same good a 'year' hence. It is only when we impose the extra condition that *money prices* should be unchanging that it becomes necessary to equate this natural rate of interest to the market rate (which is a rate of exchange between money now and money a 'year' hence). Equality between market rate and natural rate then emerges as a condition of price stability.

That was what Wicksell taught; but how is it to be generalized for an economy which is not stationary? In such an economy it will usually be true that relative prices will be varying over time, quite apart from any question of monetary disturbance. It is then impossible that there should be any rate of interest which will keep *all* money prices from

---

2 And of the second volume of the *Lectures*.
3 *Treatise on Money* (1930).
4 *Prices and Production* (1931).

changing. The most that could conceivably be stabilized would be an index number of prices, but there are many possible index numbers: does this mean that there is a different natural rate for each index number? Or should we say that, except in a stationary state, *the* natural rate of interest does not exist?

It is unnecessary even to list the further questions which arose along this line of thought (the problem of short and long rates of interest will serve as a sufficient example). For the main thing which concerns us here is that these questions could not usefully be considered at all until the Wicksell theory had been given a new look.

To make things easy, let us start by maintaining Wicksell's assumption that the underlying 'real' economy is stationary; so that 'in a condition of barter' it would in fact be stationary, or (as a money-using economy) it could be kept stationary, even with respect to money prices, by keeping the market rate equal to the natural rate. But now suppose that the market rate is reduced below the natural rate—whereat, according to Wicksell, prices will rise. But how can this happen—how can the market rate be reduced below the natural rate? And how will prices rise? What will be the time-path of the 'cumulative process'? The 'cumulative process' is not a stationary equilibrium; it is a process of change, which needs to be analysed dynamically. The questions which we have been listing are dynamic questions.

This is where we come to Lindahl. In terms of the concepts with which we are familiar, his solution can readily be described. He reduced the process of change to a sequence of single periods, such that, in the interior of each, change could be neglected. Within the single period, quantities and prices could thus be determined in what resembles a static manner. Everything is just the same as with the 'static' kind of process analysis (which we have attributed to Smith or to Marshall) save for one thing: that expectations are explicitly introduced as independent variables in the determination of the single-period equilibrium. Wicksell himself had come near to this, but it had been concealed by his habit of working with a circulating capital model. In Lindahl it is at last quite clear that the single-period is not self-contained.

The case of the cumulative process is enough to show why expectations had to be brought in. However far we go in splitting up the sequence (of stationary economy subjected to monetary disturbance), we shall still find that each single period merely reproduces the old stationary equilibrium, so long as the single period is kept self-contained, and so long as the equilibrium conditions (of demands equal to supplies) are kept in force. Everything is just the same as regards all the *real* elements in the system; and the *rate* of interest (there can be only one rate of interest) must be equal to the natural rate. Splitting up merely reduces the difference between the price levels of the successive equilibria; it does not show the transition from one equilibrium to another. Only be explicit introduction of expectations can this Eleatic paradox[5] be resolved.

What we are effectively assuming, if expectations are not introduced explicitly, is that in each single period prices are expected to remain the same in future as they are in that period; the only difference between one single period and another must then be that prices are higher in the later period, so that (if there is any hard money in the system) the demand for money must be increased. The supply of money must be increased to match this demand; so that all that has happened is that the supply of money is increased, and prices have risen. We are back at a quantity equation, buttressed by a 'real balance effect'. But this is not what Wicksell had in mind. In spite of his occasional obeisances to quantity theory orthodoxy, his most characteristic model is that of an economy in which there is no hard money, not even such as may be kept as a reserve by a Central Bank. If there is such a reserve, and we are willing to suppose that the Central Bank endeavours to keep a constant 'real balance', then (with expectations tied, as before, to current prices) we again come back to the Quantity Theory. But if there is no such reserve (or if we decline to make this special assumption about Central Bank behaviour) the position will be different—and more interesting. If there is no reserve (Wicksell's case), bank credit appears as a liability of the banking system, a debt from the banking system to the public, which is matched by debts from the public to the banking system; these can be matched *at any level*. The system can then be in equilibrium at any level of prices; there is no question of a relation between prices and the supply of money. All that is left is Wicksell's relation between prices and the rate of interest; but that is a relation that still needs to be tidied up.

---

[5] 'The moving Arrow, at an indivisible instant, must either be at rest or in motion. Now the arrow cannot move in the instant, supposed indivisible, for if it changed its position, the instant would at once be divided. If, however, it is not in motion in the instant, it must be at rest, and, as time is made up of such instants, it must always remain at rest.' (T. L. Heath, *Manual of Greek Mathematics*, p. 192.)

Let us now proceed to see how the 'cumulative process' would be analysed—on Lindahl's method.

Let period (0) be that of the old (stationary) equilibrium, with market rate equal to the natural rate, r_n. In this old equilibrium, expected prices were equal to current prices. In period (1) the monetary authority reduces the market rate of interest, and (as is agreed) prices, or at least some prices, will rise. If, however, when these prices rise, expected prices rise equally, there can be no equilibrium in period (1) until the market rate is again equal to r_n. But as soon as we allow expected prices to diverge from current prices the difficulty disappears.

The simplest rule by which a determinate *cumulative process* may then be engendered is the following. Suppose that the money prices which, in period (t), are expected to rule in all future periods $(t+1, t+2, \ldots)$ are the money prices that did actually rule in period $(t-1)$. There is a *lag* in the adjustment of expectations. Then in period (1), expected prices are (0) prices; any change in prices that occurs in (1) is taken to be temporary. There is then no difficulty in establishing, by a natural extension of static method, what will be the behaviour of the economy in (1), even though it is laid down that in (1) the rate of interest is to be reduced below r_n. If expected prices are unchanged, but the rate of interest is lower, current prices (or, at the least, some current prices) must be higher. There must be some tendency for the prices of (1) to be higher than the prices of (0). Current prices being adjusted, but expected prices not being adjusted, the rate of interest can be lower than r_n, and there can still be equilibrium.

Now pass to period (2), in which the market rate of interest is still maintained as in (1), being still less than r_n. There are just two things which can make prices in (2) different from what they were in (1). One is the fact that the system was not in stationary equilibrium in period (1)—for relative prices in (1) would not (or not all) have been the same as the stationary relative prices (of period (0)). Thus the capital stock which (2) inherits from (1) may be different from that which (1) inherited from (0). There may, that is to say, be a change in real resources. The other is the fact that, according to our rule, there will be a change in price expectations.

The prices which, in period (1), were expected to rule in the future were (0) prices; in period (2) they are (1) prices. (1) prices were, on the whole, higher than (0) prices, so that in (2) price expectations will, on the whole, be higher than they were in (1). Other things being equal, this will tend to make actual prices higher in (2) than in (1).

And other things are equal (in particular, the rate of interest is the same as it was); there is just the possible effect of the change in real resources. Apart from this, prices will be higher in (2) than in (1), and for the same reason they will be higher in (3) than in (2). The cumulative process will continue, as Wicksell said, so long as the market rate of interest is less than r_n.

But will there in fact be an offsetting effect from the change in real resources? This is a question with which Lindahl was much concerned, but it is unnecessary for me to go into it here.[6] From the point of view of the present analysis it is sufficient to observe that, even if there is such an effect, its ability to offset depends upon timing. By the 'rule' that we are using, expectations adjust themselves in one unit period; that is to say, the length of the period has been chosen so as to equal the expectational lag. The speedier the adjustment of expectations, the shorter the unit period must be. But such shortening of the unit period is bound to reduce the change in real resources that can occur within the period; for the speed of the real change is determined, at least in part, by technology—by the calendar time that production processes take. Generally, therefore, the possibility of offsetting depends upon relative speeds of adjustment in these two directions; and these speeds are largely independent of one another. If expectations are sensitive, with a short adjustment period, changes in resources cannot make much difference to the Wicksellian cumulative process. If expectations are very sluggish things may be different.

———————

I have chosen this particular example of the Lindahl method for hardly any better reason than that one had to have an example. It must, however, have been something like this line of thought that convinced Lindahl himself that expectations had to be explicitly introduced. From now on I want to consider the method more generally.

When I do so, I do not find it easy to proceed without some reference to the closely related theory which I gave myself in *Value and Capital* (based, as it was, upon conversations which I had had with Lindahl himself). The *Value and Capital* model is worked out in much greater detail than Lindahl's; for the sake of that detail I allowed

———————

[6] An increase in real capital in period (1), making possible an increase in supplies of products in period (2), may conceivably diminish the rate of interest that is appropriate for period (2), so that actual prices in (2) will fail to rise in the manner described. But in order for this to be possible at all, there must be some fixed factor (land or labour) the supply of which is not extensible to match the increase in the stock of real capital. Even so, one would surely expect that the fall would occur rather slowly.

myself a number of restrictive assumptions, some of which I have now come to think were unnecessary. I shall come back to these in later sections. It is more important, for the moment, to comment upon a point where I took a different direction from Lindahl's, under the influence (this time) of Keynes.

I was writing this part of my book in 1937–8, at a time when battle was raging over the *General Theory*. I was myself writing about Keynes in the intervals of working at my own book;[7] to clear up the relation between Keynes's approach and my own seemed (I think understandably) to be a necessary part of the task I had set myself. It had to come sooner or later, but I am now inclined to believe that I let it come too soon. I should have let my own argument develop at least one or two steps further before I looked up to see where I was in relation to the Keynes theory.

It is one of the major difficulties of the Keynes theory (as has been explained in the preceeding chapter) that it works with a *period* which is taken to be one of equilibrium (investment being equal to saving, saving that is a function of *current* income), and which is nevertheless identified with the Marshallian 'short period', in which capital equipment (now the capital equipment of the whole economy) remains unchanged. The second seems to require that the period should not be too long, but the first requires that it should not be too short; for the *process* of getting into the equilibrium in question (the multiplier process) must occupy a length of time that is by no means negligible. It is not easy to see that there can be any length of time that will adequately satisfy both of these requirements.

A reservation on this point has always, I think, been at the backs of the minds of critical readers; but we have agreed to suspend our doubts because of the power of the analysis which Keynes constructed on this shaky foundation. Once the point is granted, the way is open for the use of familiar methods (methods that differ little, in essence, from those of comparative statics), so that the state of the economy in one 'short-period equilibrium' can be compared with its state in another. For many purposes (as the whole subsequent history of the Keynes theory shows) that is all that we want.

But it is not dynamics. It is not the analysis of a process; no means has been provided by which we can pass from one Keynesian period to the next. There are indeed versions of the Keynes theory which do

---

[7] 'Mr. Keynes's Theory of Employment' (*Economic Journal*, 1936); 'Mr. Keynes and the Classics' (*Econometrica*, 1937), reprinted as essays 7 and 8 in Collected Essays II.

provide such means. The Kahn multiplier theory is a piece of dynamic analysis in the way that the Keynes multiplier theory is not. (Thus it is from the Kahn multiplier that 'Keynesian' dynamic theories commonly begin, not from the Keynes multiplier.) The Keynes theory, it has often been observed, is not a dynamic theory; in one sense, at least, it is still 'quasi-static'.

The Temporary Equilibrium model of *Value and Capital*, also, is 'quasi-static'—in just the same sense. The reason I was content with such a model was because I had my eyes fixed on Keynes.

Both the Keynes theory and the *Value and Capital* theory are dynamic to the extent that their temporary equilibrium is governed by expectations. (Keynes locked them up in the 'marginal efficiency of capital', but they are there all the same.) But they are not used in the way Lindahl used them. In Lindahl's case, as appears from our example of the cumulative process, the single periods link on. In the others, they do not. What is the difference?

The place where I myself departed from Lindahl (and so moved in the direction of Keynes) was with respect to the things which I allowed to happen within the single period. According to Lindahl (I think one may safely say) the expectations that rule in the current period are based upon *past* experience: they are uninfluenced by what happens in the market during the current period itself. It is this which enables them to form a link between periods—a link, which, once we allow them to be based on current experience, is bound to disappear.[8] It was because I did allow them to be influenced (even, on occasion, to be chiefly influenced) by current experience, that my model was moved in a 'quasi-static' direction.

It will be well, in order to explain how this happened, to go into a little more detail about the structure of the model that I was using.

During the 'week' (as I called the single period) production and consumption proceed at prices that are established by trading on its first 'day' (Monday). Monday's trading proceeds until prices are established that equate demands and supplies, for goods and services to be delivered within the 'week'. It is not supposed that equilibrium prices are established at once; there may be a good deal of 'false' trading before they are established. While they are being found, expectations are adjusting themselves to the information that comes up

---

[8] The corresponding link was dropped by Keynes when he made consumption (i.e. the output of consumption goods) depend upon *current* income.

in the course of this trading. Every change in prices, even if it is only a tentative change in prices, carries with it an adjustment of expectations; equilibrium is not established until a set of prices is reached which (together with the expectations that it engenders) determines demands and supplies that are equal to one another. This was the concept of equilibrium that I was using—made precise (indeed much too precise) by the notion of 'elasticity of expectations' (responsiveness of price expectations to current prices) which has been more of a success than I would have desired. In this equilibrium prices and price expectations are, at least to some extent, reciprocally determined.

Such reciprocal determination is, however, a piece of telescoping; in dynamic analysis, telescoping is dangerous. It is essential to keep the time-sequence right. Though changes in actual prices do affect expectations, and changes in expectations do affect actual prices, cause precedes effect. The *lag* may be short, but (in principle) it is always there. In truly dynamic analysis (of which Lindahl's is our first specimen) there must be lags.[9]

It is indeed by no means necessary that the lags should be of an expectational character (as they are in the Lindahl theory). The case of the Kahn multiplier, to which reference has already been made, is already before us as evidence to the contrary. The point which I am making is not specifically concerned with any one sort of lag; it is simply that some sort of lag is required in any dynamic theory, if process *as such* is to be made intelligible.

It is inevitable, when time is divided into single periods, that the lags should extend from one single period to another. Not necessarily from one to the next; rapidity of reaction can be varied by making the lags extend across a number of periods. The expectations of period t can be moulded, according to various possible rules, by actual experience in combinations of periods in the past. Numerous different reaction patterns can be represented in this manner; but it will usually be only very simple types that we shall care to handle.

———————

Let us go back to Lindahl. All that has been worked out, so far, is the Lindahlian approach to a very formal problem—that of Wicksell's

———

[9] This (I take it) is what Frisch meant when he defined a dynamic theory as one in which 'we consider the magnitudes of certain variables at different points of time, and we introduce certain equations which embrace at the same time several of these magnitudes belonging to different instants' ('Propagation and Impulse Problems' in *Essays in Honour of Gustav Cassel*, p. 171).

cumulative process; something must now be said about the way in which the model would deal with questions that are somewhat more realistic. We shall then not want to begin from a stationary state; and there is indeed no reason why we should. All that we have to require of our period (0) is that the system should be in temporary equilibrium in that period: that the prices that are established in that period are such as to equate supplies and demands. What these (supplies, demands, and prices) are will depend upon data—the real resources available, the tastes of 'individuals', the expectations that have been formed, and the rate of interest (supposed, as explained, to be under the control of the banking system). Production and consumption, in period (0), are then determined; and the capital equipment, which (0) will hand over to (1), is also determined. Granted a rule about the formation of expectations in period (1)—and, of course, with given tastes and so on in period (1)—the behaviour of the economy in period (1) is likewise determined. And so on for later periods.

This is a very general statement—not in itself of much use. It would not be possible to construct a 'growth model' on these lines without specifying much further. But I do not think that that was the main way in which the construction was intended to be used. After all, static theory is not ordinarily used in that way; it is not used for actual working out of the system of prices and production that corresponds to a particular set of data. The important application is to Comparative Statics—the study of the changes in production and prices which we should expect to occur when the data are changed. So it is here. The natural application of the Lindahl model is to Comparative Dynamics. We start from a *basic* Lindahl process, extending over a number of time periods, with the system (in each period) in temporary equilibrium with respect to its own data. We then ask: if the data had been changed, or amended, in some particular, how would the process have been changed? What would have been the change to the *amended* process? This, in some cases at least, is a question on which something can be said. And reflection would suggest that it is in fact one of the main questions to which we require an answer.

What has been said above about the cumulative process fits, it will be noticed, into this formulation. The basic process was in that case the stationary state with constant prices; the change in data was a change in the market rate of interest. The nature of the amended process, in that case, has been already examined. But it is now at once apparent, when we proceed to regard the 'cumulative process' analysis as an example of a general method, that essentially the same argument will apply much more generally. We can start with *any* basic process, and inquire into the consequences of reducing the market rate of interest to a lower level than it is in the basic process (it need not be constant over time in either process—it is just that the *amended* rate is below the *basic* rate in each period. If the difference in interest (in the course of interest rates) is the only difference in data between the two processes, the consequential differences must be analysable in terms of exceptional lags, and changes in real resources, as before. As before, it will follow (at least in the case where expectations are sensitive) that in the amended process, where interest rates are systematically lower, prices will rise continuously *relative* to the contemporary prices of the basic process. This will be true without our having to assume that, in either process, prices are stable. If, in the basic process, prices were stable, they would be rising in the amended process; if they had been falling in the basic process, then in the amended process they would, at least, be falling less.

Another important question, which can be dealt with in the same manner, is that of an *autonomous* change in expectations. Suppose that the only difference between the data of our two processes is that, in period (1), producers in the amended process are provided with some 'news' that makes them more optimistic (as regards price expectations) than the corresponding 'people' (also in period (1)) in the basic process. Past experience—in period (0) and its predecessors—is to be the same in both processes. What difference will be made?

It is evident that, in period (1), prices will be higher in the amended process. Accordingly, if we take it that current prices have the same (lagged) effect upon price expectations as we have hitherto been assuming, there will be (some) rise in price expectations, of a continuing character, in the amended process relatively to the basic process, even if the autonomous rise only affected the basic period. But there will then be no reason why the rise in price expectations, and the consequential rise in actual prices, should increase over time. Temporary optimism (at constant market rate of interest, and with the effect on real resources—real accumulation of capital—still neglected) will result in a *permanent* lift in the price level, relative to that of the basic process; but it will not result in a continuing rise, relative to the price level of the basic process.

An autonomous 'improvement' in expectations, that does persist from period to period, can of course be treated as a sequence of temporary 'improvements'. Thus on the same analysis, it *will* result in a continuing rise in prices, relative to the price level of the basic process.

The analysis of the preceding section is important. We shall come back to it again, in other forms, in other contexts. But for the moment it is important to realize its limitations—what it does *not* give us. It is generally true of the Temporary Equilibrium method, as so far expounded, that it has serious defects, in at least three distinguishable directions. Some of these defects may be mendable to some extent; but their combined force is such that they make it impossible for us to rest content with the Temporary Equilibrium method as our only dynamic method. It is necessary, as we shall see in detail in later chapters, to have alternative approaches at our disposal as well.

The first of the defects which I shall consider concerns uncertainty. My 1939 analysis has often been criticized (and the same criticism could, I think, be directed against Lindahl's analysis) for its neglect of uncertainty, or rather for its inadequate treatment of uncertainty. Far more is known now than was known then about 'decision-making under uncertainty' (Theory of Games and all that!); what it is that is left out, on the uncertainty side, can now be more accurately defined.[10]

An uncertain expectation (of the price of a commodity, we may still allow ourselves to say, that is to rule at some future date) can be represented (more or less adequately) by a probability distribution; and this (in turn) is usually describable by a fairly small number of parameters. These may be the ordinary statistical parameters (mean value, variance, and so on); or it may be that there are others more appropriate to the particular matter in hand.[11] The important thing is that an uncertain expectation cannot be adequately described in terms of a single parameter. It is insufficient to consider the changes in production (or consumption) plans that result from changes in the prices that are 'expected' as most probable. Attention must also be given to the effects of changes in the confidence with which these values are expected.

[10] Discussions of the uncertainty problem that are rather closely fitted to the *Value and Capital* analysis are to be found in A. G. Hart, *Anticipations, Uncertainty and Dynamic Planning*; and in F. Modigliani and K. J. Cohen, *Role of Anticipations and Plans in Economic Behaviour*.

[11] As Professor Shackle would have us believe.

When these are allowed for, the theory of the 'plan' becomes much more complicated; for it is necessary to take account of those adjustments in business organization which are undertaken in order to diminish risk—and which otherwise are only too likely to slip through our fingers.[12] But the temporary equilibrium itself would not appear, at first sight, to be much affected. Current prices (or, more generally, the character of the equilibrium that is established in the current period) may affect future planning by their effect on the confidence with which expectations are held, as well as by their effect on the most probable expected prices. But though that is a bother in the statement of the theory, it looks as if it could be worked in without too much trouble, and without changing much that is of substance.

What, however, about the rate of interest? This is where there is a real and important difference. So long as we assume (as we have hitherto been implicitly assuming) that expectations are single-valued, we can talk, as we have done, about a *single* rate of interest. It is indeed possible (as was shown in *Value and Capital*) to deal with differences in the rate of interest on loans of different maturities. This can be done (the method there adopted) by reducing long lending to a sequence of short lendings—so that a long rate is regarded as being compounded out of *the* short rate and a succession of expected rates); or it can be done (as many people would prefer to do it) by taking the longest of long rates to be *the* rate, and regarding short lending as long lending which is planned to be undone at the end of the period. So long as expectations are single-valued, there is no inherent difference in these methods. In either case, there is one rate of interest which is *the* rate of interest in the current period.

As soon as we allow for uncertainty of expectation, such simple reductions fail us. They fail us in two ways. First, because of default risk, there will be no uniformity in the rates of interest that are established, as the same time, even on loans of the same maturity. Secondly (and more importantly), the amount that a business can borrow, at *any* fixed rate of interest, will be limited by its *credit*; but this barrier can be relaxed, to an extent which varies greatly with confidence, by the raising of funds in other manners, on equities and the like. If these things were to be fully allowed for, the Temporary Equilibrium model would require considerable amendment—a formidable task that has never (to my knowledge) been seriously carried

---

[12] Hart, op.cit.; G. B. Richardson, *Information and Investment*, ch. 8.

through.[13] I shall not attempt it here, but shall merely mention one fairly obvious point which emerges as soon as one begins to think about the matter.

In the Temporary Equilibrium model, as we have been describing it, the rate of interest is under the control of the Monetary Authority. But as soon as we admit the existence of a spectrum of interest rates (and 'pseudo' interest rates, such as expected yields on equities) the direct control of the monetary authority over interest must be limited to a part (perhaps a quite small part) of the spectrum. How far the rest of the spectrum can be influenced depends not so much on arithmetical relations between rates—the extent to which one comes down just because another does may be infinitesimal; it is a matter of backwashes on confidence that do not proceed by any simple rule. We may still derive from the theory some useful knowledge of the way in which interest changes will affect production and prices, if they can be carried through; but we must not assume that they can always be carried through just because the monetary authority desires it.

The second of the limitations which I want to discuss (but perhaps it is only a limitation of the *Value and Capital* model) is the confinement to the case of perfect competition. *Value and Capital* was of course throughout a perfect-competition book; it was confined to the study of the pure theory of the perfect-competition model. In such a model prices are the variables on which the working of the whole economy depends; supplies and demands are functions of prices. When expectations are introduced into analysis of this sort, it is natural to introduce them as price expectations. Supplies and demands have been taken to be dependent (statically) upon current prices; dynamically they should be dependent upon expected prices also.

Even in the present chapter (though I have not been supposing myself to be referring so expressly to the perfect competition model) I have allowed myself to drop into this familiar representation of expectations as *price* expectations; this is indeed very often a convenient simplification, but I do not think that it need be any more than that. There is no reason in principle why we should not have a Temporary Equilibrium theory of Imperfect Competition, in which the prices at which the firm sells are not independent of the quantities that it offers for sale. What it must then 'expect' is not a price, but a

---

[13] It has not been carried through formally, but it can still be used, as I have done myself in some of the writings listed in the note at the end of the proceeding chapter.

relation between quantities and prices (demand curve or demand function). It is this which will be determined from outside, when it becomes actual, and must in the meantime be estimated from such evidence as there is.

The simplest (but not the most interesting) form of this dynamic Imperfect Competition theory would make expected demand, in each future period, depend upon the price to be fixed in that future period, but on nothing else that was under the control of the seller. The forms which such a relation could take might then be sufficiently distinguished by the values of quite a small number of parameters (if the 'curve' were linear, or log-linear, two would suffice). Changes in these parameters would then correspond exactly to the change in price expectations of the Perfect Competition theory. We could substitute these parameters for the price expectations; otherwise we should proceed in almost the same way as we have done before.

The interesting form of the theory, however, is more complex. It is not in general to be expected that the price fixed in any period will affect sales in that period alone; if 'news' takes time to travel, the price in one period will affect sales in later periods also. Demand functions, that is, will be temporally interrelated. It is then more difficult to reduce demand behaviour into terms of changes in a small number of parameters. In order to make the problem manageable, we are likely to have to confine ourselves to the study of simple cases. Some of these, however, seem to be by no means uninstructive.[14]

Neither of the two limitations, so far discussed, is inherent; either can be removed, or partially removed, if we are willing to take the trouble to do so; but the third, to which I now come, is inherent in the Temporary Equilibrium method itself. Both in the Lindahl version and in the *Value and Capital* version (and in the version given to this chapter, if that is to be distinguished from them) it is necessary to assume that prices remain unchanged throughout the single period; and that these prices are equilibrium prices which, within the single period, equate supplies and demands. In order to visualize this, some such construction as my 'week' and my 'Monday' appears to be necessary; but the artificiality of such constructions is only too obvious. They do deliberate violence to the *order* in which in the real world (in *any* real world) events occur.

[14] A particularly simple case of this kind is explored in my article *The Process of Imperfect Competition* (Oxford Economic Papers, 1954), reprinted as 'Stickers and Snatchers' in *Collected Essays* III.

It is no doubt true that the violence is greater with some market forms than it is with others. Though the Lindahl theory sprang from Wicksell, its conception of the working of the market is essentially Marshallian (in the *Value and Capital* version, the Marshallian affiliation is made explicit). We (Lindahl and I) were following Marshall in treating prices as determined (in the short period, or single period) by 'equilibrium of demand and supply'. Our single period (or 'week') was shorter than Marshall's 'short period'; this made the equilibrium assumption still more dangerous. Marshall, it was argued above,[15] may have been justified in the use that he made of it, in 1890; but to continue with it in the nineteen-thirties, and to make an even stronger use of it, was very dangerous indeed.

One of the reasons for this is that which came to be emphasized by Keynes: that there are markets, especially the labour market, in which prices are 'sticky'. The assumption of demand and supply equality, in every period, must for such markets be peculiarly unsatisfactory. In Keynesian terms, the Temporary Equilibrium theory is a full-employment theory. But this is not all. There are many non-labour markets, in which Temporary Equilibrium gives a wrong impression of the market's working, in which it does not tell the story right. As a consequence, it leaves out parts of the dynamic problem in which we have a right to be interested. We have got to find some way of dealing with them.

Lindahl himself came to recognize this; in his later work he moved away from the Temporary Equilibrium method. In my own later work (and not only in this book[16]) I have done the same. But I do not wish to relinquish it entirely. I have not presented it here as an historical curiosity. For, as I have repeatedly insisted, it is not enough to have an economics which is committed to some particular market form; even if it is the form which happens to be dominant at the time, and in the country, in which we are living. We need something more than that. As a theory of its own market form the Temporary Equilibrium method is valid enough. But that is not all that there is to be said.

For one thing, even in the twentieth century there are markets (speculative markets in particular) which do work in a way that is near enough to what has been described. If we cannot give ourselves up to the Temporary Equilibrium model we can make some use of it as an ingredient. This is indeed what Keynes did, in the 'LM' part of

---

15 pp. 49–50.
16 In my *Trade Cycle* (1950) I did not use the Temporary Equilibrium method.

the *General Theory*. When he determined his rate of interest by supply of money and liquidity preference, he was using a much simplified Temporary Equilibrium model. It is still such a model which we need for the analysis of financial markets, even if we do not follow him in making his simplications.

There is another thing too. Throughout this chapter I have been discussing the Temporary Equilibrium method as a method of Positive Economics—Pure Positive Economics it may be (to revert to the distinction which I made in Chapter 1) but Positive Economics all the same. What about Welfare Economics? The supply–demand equalization, which has been causing us such disquiet, when it is taken as a characteristic of a Positive Economic model, is, when it comes to Welfare Economics, perfectly at home.[17] If we are studying the properties of an optimum growth path, one of the things on which we shall insist is that, in each single period, it is to be in temporary equilibrium; and in this application even the other 'limitations' of the simple Temporary Equilibrium model (risklessness and perfect competition) may actually be found to be acceptable. If we are concerned with Welfare Economics, the Temporary Equilibrium model, or something very like it, should be just what we want.

And not temporary equilibrium only. What, it may be asked, has happened in the foregoing to an equilibrium that is more than temporary? Is there no equilibrium over time, equilibrium over a sequence of single periods, here at all? Temporary equilibrium is such that all are reaching their 'best' positions, subject to the constraints by which they are bound, and with the expectations that they have at the moment. Equilibrium over time, if it is to be defined in a corresponding manner, must be such that it is maintainable over a sequence, the expectations on which it is based, in each single period, being consistent with one another. When it is described as an 'equilibrium of perfect foresight', this equilibrium over time may hardly appear to be an interesting concept. But when it is looked at the other way, as a means of studying the properties of an optimum growth path, it may possibly appear to be less of a chimera.

A further Note on Lindahl

I have come to feel, on rereading this chapter, that it still looks at Lindahl too much from the standpoint of the *Value and Capital* model. So

---

[17] The qualifications about free goods, on which the 'linear programmers' (rightly) insist, do not here concern us.

the version which I give, though I do not in any way withdraw it, is not quite fair to Lindahl. For I have left out one aspect to which he attached great importance. It is the link between his monetary theory, alone so far considered, and his other main interest—in Social Accounting.

The part that has been played by Social Accounting in the development of Keynesian theory has already concerned us, and will again concern us later; it may indeed be said, both for Keynes and for Lindahl, that the introduction of accounting procedure into economics was one of their chief innovations. Neither of them paid much attention to what was to go on *within* the single-period; each of them held that the performance of the period could be adequately represented by its accounts. But while Keynes's accounting structure was taken from business accounting (an income-expenditure account and a balance-sheet), Lindahl's was taken from public finance. He had begun as a specialist in public finance before he turned to money, so it is was natural for him to look there for his apparatus.

Government accounting has two features that distinguish it. One is the fact that governments are not obliged by any company law to present balance-sheets; it is nearly always true that their only account is an income-expenditure account. The other is that, unlike businesses, governments do not merely present a running account for the year that is closing, they also present a quite formal *forward* account—of the expenditure planned, and the revenue expected, for the ensuing year. Both of these persist in the Lindahl theory. The balance-sheet drops into the background; but great stress is laid on the distinction between forward and backward accounts—*ex ante* and *ex post.*

The story of the 'cumulative process' could be restated in these terms, as Lindahl would himself have preferred to state it, without any fundamental change. In period (0), that of the stationary equilibrium, realized prices are the same as those expected; *ex ante* and *ex post* are the same. In period (1) *ex ante* prices are the same as in period (0), save that the rate of interest is reduced. In consequence of that the *ex post* prices, in this same period (1), are higher. These *ex post* prices of period (1) are carried forward to be the *ex ante* prices of period (2); and so on. All of the accounts, *ex ante* and *ex post* for each period, can be written in those terms.

It does perhaps become a little clearer, in the light of this restatement, that the model, as so far described, is what it is convenient to call a *flexprice* model. Prices, *ex post* prices, are determined—all of

them, with the exception of the rate of interest—by equilibrium of demand and supply. There is no place for rigidity of prices—or wages.
That was Lindahl's first model; but he later became dissatisfied with
it. He sought to introduce some rigidity of prices; so he had to throw
his *ex ante ex post* disequilibrium on to the side of quantities. Much the
same as happened over those same years with Keynes.

It is unlikely to have been the influence of Keynes which first moved
Lindahl in that direction, for there was a similar development nearer
his home. Myrdal, in his *Monetary Equilibrium*, to which I referred in
the note at the beginning of this chapter, had begun, rather formally,
with criticism of Wicksell. It was he who first showed, expressly, that
the definition of the natural rate of interest as that which would be
determined in a barter economy (one of the definitions given by
Wicksell) made no sense except in a stationary state. If relative prices
are changing, there will be a different natural rate in this sense for
each commodity. Thus one has to fall back on a definition by effect on
the movement of some price-level. But what price-level? There can be
nothing more than a conventional answer, if prices are perfectly flexible. But if some prices are less flexible than others, the best that can
be done for stability (for 'Monetary Equilibrium') is to stabilize, so
far as possible, the rigid prices, that is to avoid setting a strain
on the rigid prices, which would put those markets into supply-
demand disequilibrium. That clearly leads, in practice, to something
very like the 'full employment' of Keynes. Myrdal had got there,
before he can have seen the *General Theory*.

It may be useful to remark, before leaving the matter, that the
accounting structure that was used by Lindahl does have some continuing merits; so it is rather unfortunate that in later thinking it has
been so largely disregarded. The social accounting that has now so
long been, in many countries, official is Keynesian in inspiration; it is
an effort to force the accounting of the whole economy into the form
of business accounts. How unsuitable that is for the accounting of the
public sector we now have much experience to show. In this field at
least, it may still be contended, *ex ante ex post* remains respectable.[18]

[18] It is used, in a manner which (I hope and believe) is quite in Lindahl's spirit, in a
recent paper of my own on capital gains, in relation to taxation (Collected Essays III
pp. 189–203).

8

THE FIXPRICE METHOD

The fundamental weakness of the Temporary Equilibrium method, if we keep it as our only dynamic method, is the assumption, which it is bound to make, that markets are in equilibrium—actual demand the same as desired demand, actual supply the same as desired supply —even in the very short period, which is what its single-period must be taken to be. This assumption comes down from Marshall, but even in a very competitive economy such very short-run equilibration is hard to swallow; in relation to modern manufacturing industry, it is hard to swallow indeed. It was inevitable that the time should come when it had to be dropped.

The consequences of dropping it make quite a revolution. It is a revolution which is often mixed up with the so-called 'Keynesian revolution', but it is better to keep them apart. In the model of the *General Theory* there is just one market, the labour market, which is out of equilibrium; it is when we decide to admit the possibility of disequilibrium in other markets that we need a new method. Labour market disequilibrium can be treated, as Keynes treated it, statically or quasi-statically; but in other markets, especially product markets, it has different characteristics, which (as we shall see) are inherently dynamic.

Though the new method is not in the *General Theory*, it is in work that was based upon it that the beginnings are to be found. And one can see how that was, how it had to be. Consider a question which must have occurred to many readers: why is there not in Keynes's later book, a chapter on external trade? There had been plenty about that in the *Treatise*, but in the *General Theory* it is curiously missing. What would have happened if Keynes had tried to put it in? He could not have avoided attention to a condition of equilibrium, which in that context must have been of fundamental importance—nothing else but the balancing of external payments. In the closed economy of the *General Theory* there is no room for it; but why is there no room for it? Is there not something analogous to it which might, or should, have found a place?

This is a question which could not have been answered without bringing back the stocks and work-and-progress, which got much attention in the *Treatise*, but which in the *General Theory* have so oddly disappeared. When the balance of external payments is balanced, the stock of foreign exchange, at the disposal of the monetary authority, meets its requirements, or is 'normal'. To carry over a similar concept to the rest of the economy we have to make it a condition of equilibrium that stocks and work-in-progress, over the rest of the economy, should be normal. But we cannot do that unless we admit some element of sticky prices.

If exchange rates are perfectly flexible, so we have often been told, the balance of payments must balance. If prices are perfectly flexible, can there be surpluses or deficiencies in stocks? There is this line of thought which leads from Keynes to our new method, but doubtless there are others also.

———————

I shall begin by taking the new method in rather a stark form. In that form it is sharply contrasted with the Temporary Equilibrium method; more sharply, perhaps, than we shall ultimately desire it to be. I do not think that there is any harm in this. The Temporary Equilibrium method, as I have expounded it, was itself a pure method, in which all markets were supposed to work in the same way—a way which may be realistic for some markets, but which is certainly not realistic for many. We shall best get a grip on the alternative method if we start by taking it also in a pure form. Though our ultimate preference may be for some combination, some markets working one way and some the other, any such mixed model must partake to some extent of the difficulties of both approaches. It is the extremes which are relatively simple, so with them it is best to begin.

On the Temporary Equilibrium method the system is in equilibrium in every single period, and it is by this equilibrium that prices are determined. If we abandon the demand–supply equation, how are prices to be determined? The answer, which must be faced, is that the new method does not have any way of determining prices. There must be some way by which they are determined, but it is exogenous. The determination of prices is taken right outside the model.[1]

All that is said about prices is that they must cover costs; more strictly, that a thing will not be produced unless it is profitable to produce it. Subject to this condition, prices can be what they like. It is not a very stringent condition, if it is unaccompanied by any rule

———

[1] 'Cost Push', with prices ultimately set by trade unions, is thus an hypothesis that fits very neatly into a model of this kind.

about profits being normal; and the normalization of profits (equalization between different sectors) is a complicated process, for which it is difficult to give sufficient time during the lapse of a single period.

If there is no more than that to be said about prices, it is natural to assume that they remain unchanged throughout the sequence that is being analysed. If prices are fixed exogenously, one will naturally begin by assuming them to be constant. The model becomes a Fixprice model. Fixity of prices is in fact the characteristic feature of the models to which we now come, so characteristic that it will be convenient to use it as a name for the method. (The Temporary Equilibrium method can then be referred to, by contrast, as a Flexprice method.) It must be emphasized that it is not implied by the description Fixprice method that prices are never to be allowed to change—only that they do not necessarily change whenever there is demand–supply disequilibrium.

When prices are constant, quantities of goods and services can be added by adding their money values; money values become volume indexes. By its own inner logic, and without any deliberate decision having been taken to slew it in that direction, the model becomes a macro-model. The Fixprice method has an inherent tendency to 'go macro'; a tendency which there is now much experience to confirm.

It would, however, be unwise to rush too quickly into macroeconomics. If a model of the whole economy is to be securely based, it must be grounded in an intelligible account of how a single market is supposed to work. What is the Fixprice theory of the working of a single market? In what ways does it differ from a Flexprice theory, such (for instance) as Marshall's?

The standard case of Marshallian micro-theory (as previously noticed)[2] assumes that the traded commodity is non-storable ('fish') so that there can be no carry-over from one period to another. This is not, in practice, a particularly important case; the products of manufacturing industry, at least, do commonly have a greater durability; but it has been handed down from textbook to textbook as a standard case, merely because, in Flexprice terms, it is easy to handle. Having once got that case clear, one can go on to work out the Flexprice theory of a storable commodity without essential change in principle. When price is rigid, the advantage of beginning in this way is,

[2] pp. 48–9.

however, less obvious. The existence of stocks has a great deal to do, in practice, with the possibility of keeping prices fixed. If, when demand exceeds output, there are stocks that can be thrown in to fill the gap, it is obvious that the price does not have to rise; a market in which stock changes substitute for price changes (at least up to a point) is readily intelligible. If there are no stocks to take the strain, it is harder to stick to the assumption of rigid prices. A market in which sellers leave demand unsatisfied without raising prices is certainly not a 'perfect' market—but it is quite a familiar sort of market in the real world all the same! The Fixprice assumption is more awkward in the case of non-storable than in that of storable commodities; but it is an assumption which even there we can bring ourselves, at least provisionally, to accept.

Let us therefore begin by reminding ourselves of Marshall's story. The price that actually rules for a perishable, price-flexible commodity of Marshall's type is that which equates current demand with current output. The commodity being perishable, the supply cannot include any stock element (positive or negative); it is 'flow demand' and 'flow supply' that are equated at the price that is established. If, however, they are only equated at a high price (at a price that is high relative to 'normal cost of production') there is a signal for an increase in output; though the increase can only materialize at a later date—that is to say, in a later period. If they are equated at a price that is low in relation to cost, output will (similarly) tend to decrease. That is what we read in Marshall, or (indeed) in Adam Smith.

Now suppose that the price is rigid. There is then no reason why demand and supply (or output) should be equated—should be in equilibrium—in the current period. The commodity being perishable, an excess of demand over output cannot be met from stocks; it must simply go unsatisfied. An excess of output over demand cannot be added to stocks; it must simply be wasted. But that is not all that there is to be said. An excess of demand over output will still give the same sort of signal to increase future output—for we are assuming that if output can be sold, it will be profitable to produce it; an excess of output over demand still gives a signal to contract. Even in a Fixprice market the signalling does occur. The economy is not deprived of a means of adjustment, at least so far as the 'micro' level is concerned. If producers read the signals correctly (and even in the Flexprice market they still need to read the signals correctly) there can still be a 'tendency to equilibrium'.

When stocks are carried, the position is more complicated—much more complicated. For in that case (as we shall see in detail later[3]) it is not sufficient that producers should *on the whole* read the signals correctly. A fair adjustment of flow output to flow demand is not sufficient to ensure a fair adaptation to equilibrium. Exact adjustment cannot be expected; mistakes are bound to be made; but whereas in the case of the non-storable commodity mistakes are not carried forward, in the case of the storable commodity they are. Even a mere lag in adjustment (and the absence of any lag is hardly conceivable) will leave its mark upon the level of stocks. Thus, as soon as we allow for carry-forward of stocks, the problem of equilibration in a Fixprice model is fundamentally transformed. We may express the transformation, at least provisionally, by saying that we do not only have to attend to the flow equilibrium of current demand and current output; we must also attend to the question of stock equilibrium.

The concept of 'stock equilibrium' is becoming familiar to economists;[4] but to give a general definition of it is by no means a simple matter. There is a crying need for such a definition if we are to make orderly progress in Fixprice theory; the matter needs a thorough investigation, so that I propose to give it a chapter to itself. It will, however, be useful, before we proceed to that inquiry, to look once again at the 'micro-model' of the single market. For there is one way in which our discussion of it may have given a wrong impression. By looking at the single market so much in isolation, we have failed to bring out how central, for all Fixprice analysis, the concept of stock equilibrium really is. If we had looked at the same story in a wider way we should have found that we could not do without stock equilibrium, even if we began by considering the market for a perishable good.

Suppose that demand for butter has exceeded output of butter, and there are no stocks, so that butter, which people would have been willing to purchase, could not be bought. How will these consumers react? (There is no problem of the sellers' reaction, beyond that on their decisions to undertake future production; this we have already taken into account.) But what about the buyers? Their obvious reaction is to go away and buy something else. It is conceivable that this

---

[3] Especially in Chapter 10 below.
[4] It is sufficient to cite the 'portfolio equilibrium' of Liquidity Preference theory as an example.

may be the whole answer. If the consumers had simply shifted their demands, requiring more butter and less of other perishables, they may just be obliged to go back to those other perishables; they may just be unable to shift their demand in the way that they desired. They are obliged to substitute, for the things they wanted, things which are in more abundant supply.

There is a further possibility, which in a full analysis must be included. Suppose that the unsatisfied demand cannot be shifted at all, since there are no available supplies of substitute commodities, either from stocks or from current output. The only thing that can then be done with the money that cannot be spent is to carry it forward. But the carrying-forward of unspent balances, when their owners would have wished to spend them, and do not desire to carry them forward, is the same kind of thing as occurs on the other side, when supplies that a seller desired to sell could not be sold. The seller is left with stocks that he does not desire to hold; the consumer (or buyer) is left with money that he does not desire to keep—in exactly the same sense. In both cases there is the same kind of stock disequilibrium.

Having got so far, let us look back at the case of the seller with the perishable product, who, if demand does not come up to expectations, has to 'waste' it or throw it away. We have said that in this case the disequilibrium is not carried forward. If we are solely considering the market for the product, that is correct; but if we widen our view, as we have just been doing in considering the consumer's position, it is not correct. Goods have been produced which could not be sold; the funds that were invested in those goods must therefore have been lost. What this means, in balance-sheet terms, is that the producer is left with a debt (or liability) against which there is no corresponding asset —a debt which he presumably owes to the same creditor to whom he owed it initially, for it is not the debt that has changed, it is the asset that has disappeared. Accordingly, just as we found (on the other side of the market) that there were 'surplus' money balances in the hands of consumers—debts owing to them which they did not desire at that time to have owing to them—so in this case we have a corresponding debt owed by producers, a debt which they do not (now) willingly assume, for there is no productive asset corresponding to it.

That, of course, is not the end of the story; it is indeed the main point that it is not the end of the story. Any economic entity which is left in a state of disequilibrium will take steps to right that disequilibrium; that is the characteristic effect of disequilibrium; it is the way in which disequilibrium carries its effect down the sequence. In this particular case, moderate losses can be offset by a reduction in dividends (or other withdrawals); that is one way in which the disequilibrium can be corrected (from the firm's point of view). It is, however, convenient not to rush on, so as to bring the reduction in dividend into the same period as that in which the loss is incurred. For we can then say that a demand–supply inequality, in the period in which it occurs, always shows itself in someone's stock (or balance-sheet) disequilibrium. There is great theoretical convenience to be got from unifying our treatment by adhering to this principle. And, after all, it is not an unrealistic convention: there is commonly quite a lag between the in-curring of losses and the cutting of dividends (or, in worse cases, the 'reconstruction') that follows.

A general framework for Fixprice analysis is now beginning to show itself. Though we no longer assume that the system is in equilibrium in every single period, it could be in equilibrium (in some sense) under appropriate conditions; the conditions under which it could be in equilibrium are no less worthy of study than they were before. It is, however, impossible to deduce the actual path of the economy from a knowledge of these equilibrium conditions, and nothing more. The equilibrium conditions do not determine the actual path; all that they determine (or the most that they can determine) is an equilibrium path that we can use as a standard of reference. There will always be deviations from the equilibrium path. Some of these are simply due to imperfect planning (lack of foresight). But once a deviation has occur-red, it leaves those affected in a state of stock disequilibrium; and their endeavours to right that disequilibrium are a main determinant of the next steps on the actual path. They are not the only deter-minant; the usual static propensities and technical restraints, all the things that are alone at work on the equilibrium path, are also pre-sent. It is, however, of the greatest importance to distinguish these two elements, which work in a distinctly different manner.[5] The 'equilibrium' forces are (relatively) dependable; the 'disequilibrium' forces are much less dependable. We can invent rules for their work-ing, and calculate the behaviour of the resulting models; but such calculations are of illustrative value only. This is where 'states of

---

[5] See also p. 141 above. In many cycle theories (including my own *Contribution to the Theory of the Trade Cycle*) these two elements are quite insufficiently distinguished.

mind' are of dominating importance; and states of mind cannot readily be reduced to rule.

These are things that will be worked out in some detail in the following chapters. Their full significance will only appear when they have been worked out. In the meantime what has been said may be useful as giving some indication of the way we are going.

9

STOCKS AND FLOWS

The point has now arrived at which we must attempt a definition (a general definition) of the concept of stock equilibrium.[1] It is evident that this is going to be a key point of the Fixprice theory to which we have now come.

Stock equilibrium is an equilibrium at a point of time; in accounting terms, it is an equilibrium of the balance-sheet. That sounds simple; but the balance-sheet of a business, even as it is in practice, is quite a peculiar construction. It is important to realize that its counterpart in economic theory is also a peculiar construction, in much the same way.

The solid information on which a firm's accounts are constructed consists in records of the actual purchases and sales that it makes, goods and services that have actually been acquired or disposed of at prices that have been recorded. The 'transactions' or 'cash book' account that includes all such transactions over a period, and nothing else, is the unanalysed account from which the accountant starts. To that account the balance-sheet is in strong contrast. At the point of time to which the balance-sheet refers, the items that figure upon it are being held by the firm—that is to say, they are *not* being exchanged. Some may be near to being exchanged; they may have been recently purchased, or may be intended to be sold in the near future; values that are reasonably secure may then be placed upon them. (It should, however, be noticed that even in these cases these values are not necessarily firm values; an article may lose value very rapidly after it has been purchased; an expectation of sale, even in the near future, is not the same thing as an actual sale.) More importantly, perhaps, there are some assets (liquid assets) which are effectively identical with things (including securities) that are currently being bought and sold by others; they have a firm *market* price. Characteristically, however, the values that are set upon the items (the positive and even the negative items) in a balance-sheet are not firm figures. They are

---

[1] A point which (the reader may have noticed) was missing from our general discussion of the concept of equilibrium in Chapter 2.

estimates, accountant's estimates, of a different *quality* from the items in the transactions account, which can normally be taken to be *firm*.

This distinction—this eminently practical distinction—between transactions accounting and balance-sheet accounting reflects itself in dynamic theory. The items on which a firm makes its practical decisions are the transactions items; a theory which is solely concerned with these voluntary decisions had better run, so far as it can, in terms of transactions alone. That, essentially, is what we do—what we find ourselves doing—in a Temporary Equilibrium theory. That theory can be set out (as it was in Chapter 7, above, and as it was in *Value and Capital*) without attention to balance-sheets—without accordingly, any specific mention of stocks and flows. As long as we hold to the principle of price determination by 'equilibrium of demand and supply', on which that theory is based, we have no call to attend to anything but transactions. We do not need to distinguish between stocks and flows; for stocks and flows enter into the determination of equilibrium in exactly the same way.

There can, in competitive conditions, be no more than one price for the same commodity at the same time; and even in conditions that are only partially competitive, it does not have one price as stock and another as flow. The supply and the demand that are equated, in the single period of Temporary Equilibrium theory, may (and probably will) contain stock elements as well as flow elements. Supply comes partly from stock carried over, partly from new production; demand is partly a demand for use, partly a demand for carry-forward. Expectations of future prices affect both elements; interest affects both elements. The analysis does not require that stock and flow should be separated into compartments. It is not the case that there is one stock equilibrium and one flow equilibrium. There is one 'stock–flow' equilibrium of the single period; and that is all.[2]

The essential difference, when we pass to Fixprice theory, is that the position in which the firm finds itself at a point of time (at significant points of time) does not have to be a position that is *chosen*. It is the position which would have been chosen that is the equilibrium

[2] It follows that when one is using the Temporary Equilibrium method, the capital–income (or stock–flow) distinction is irrelevant; one can bring it in if one chooses, but any reasons there can be for doing this must be extraneous to the model itself. I found this, in my own experience, while I was writing *Value and Capital*; so I relegated the concept of income to a separate, and logically dispensable, chapter (XIV). This was entirely correct, in terms of the Temporary Equilibrium method, which I was there using; but of course I did not then realize, as I have later realized, the scope of the other method where it does belong.

position; the divergence from that measures the extent of disequilibrium. The important thing is the extent of disequilibrium at the end of the single period—at the junction, that is, between one single period and the next.

That is why it is that in Fixprice theory we do have to use the concept of stock equilibrium; for it is by the absence of stock equilibrium that disequilibrium itself is carried forward. And it is the carrying-forward of disequilibrium which is the interesting thing. If it were possible for disequilibrium to be confined within the single period, its existence would do no more than mark a failure to attain a static optimum; we could say all we had to say about it by static methods. It has, however, been shown (in the preceding chapter) that even in the simplest conceivable cases it cannot be so confined. It will always leave a trail behind it. The way in which it hands itself on to the succeeding period is by leaving the firm (or other unit) and therefore the economy, at the junction, in a state of stock disequilibrium.

It is clearly desirable that our definition of 'stock equilibrium' should be usable (or as usable as possible) in Flexprice as in Fixprice theory; but we shall not be surprised to find that it is in Fixprice theory that the concept is more at home. Let us begin by getting it into a form which is suitable for Fixprice theory; and then see how much of it we can keep for the other case.

It is tempting to say that a firm is in stock (or balance-sheet) equilibrium if the assets (the physical assets) that it holds, the debts that it owes, and the debts (including money) that are owing to it, form a combination that is in some sense the best out of alternative combinations. But what alternatives? Any balance-sheet change (purchase or sale of assets, raising of new credits, and even repayment of old) takes time to arrange: how are such changes to be made 'at a point of time'? If 'point of time' is taken strictly, there can be no alternative to what is actual. So, at first, one is tempted to argue; but this is a form of argument which is appropriate to Flexprice, not to Fixprice, theory. If the actual position may be a disequilibrium position, it is not necessarily one that has been voluntarily taken. It is itself not necessarily a *chosen* position; the alternatives to it are not choices that could have been made but are rejected. They must be alternatives in some other sense.

The fact is that in following the accountants in looking at the balance-sheet alone, we are (like the accountants) abstracting. We are deliberately looking at a part, not at the whole, of the firm's (or other unit's) position. The alternatives are not alternatives that are now available, nor do they even define alternatives that might have been available if in the past some different policy had been followed. They are simply the alternative balance-sheets (supposing actual physical assets to be listed on the balance-sheet) which, at current prices, would show the same 'net worth'. ('Net worth' is simply the balance of assets over liabilities—nominal 'liabilities', such as those that the firm owes to its own shareholders, being of course excluded.) One may perhaps say that they are the alternatives that 'look as if they were available' when one considers the balance-sheet alone—the balance-sheet *in itself*.

The use of such a concept as this in a Flexprice theory will evidently present difficulties—confirming our suspicion that stock equilibrium is not a concept that in a Flexprice theory it will often be convenient to use. In fact, it is only usable in such theory to a very limited extent. There are some balance-sheet changes (changes that only affect the more 'liquid' end of the balance-sheet) which, though they take some time to arrange, do not take much time; so that the time which is taken for them may justifiably (for appropriate purposes) be neglected. It is then permissible to say (as in Liquidity Preference and such-like 'portfolio equilibrium' theories one does say) that, so far as this part of the balance-sheet is concerned, a unit will be all the time (or practically all the time) in stock equilibrium. But it is much more difficult to extend such analysis to the whole of the balance-sheet. For if changes take time, and prices may change during that time, the line between 'capital' and 'income' becomes hard to draw. We cannot firmly separate 'capital' from 'income' items unless we have begun by solving the baffling problem of 'maintaining capital—*real* capital—intact'.

In Fixprice theory there is no such difficulty. The fixing of prices gives a firm line between capital and income. The alternative balance-sheets are simply alternative forms in which the capital of the unit (or its 'net worth') might *apparently* be held. A change from one to another is an exchange of equal value (at the ruling prices) for equal value. But because the system is a disequilibrium system, such exchanges cannot necessarily be made. At the best they take time. The comparison between the 'alternatives' is nevertheless significant. For if the situation of the unit is in this sense one of stock disequilibrium, we may assume that it will endeavour to get out of that disequilibrium, when and as it can.

_____

A firm is in stock equilibrium if its balance-sheet is the 'best' of such alternative balance-sheets; but what do we mean by 'best'? A firm is a producing unit; 'best' must be best with respect to plans and expectations. The equilibrium balance-sheet is that which is most appropriate to expectations—in one or other of the senses in which we have used that term.

In Temporary Equilibrium theory (where, as explained, the concept of stock equilibrium can only be applied at all conveniently if its application is restricted to the more liquid end of the balance-sheet) expectations will, as usual, be price expectations; expectations of yields, interest rates, and so on. The equilibrium balance-sheet is that which gives the most favourable expectation of yield (with allowance for risk). This, I think, is in full accordance with usual practice in Liquidity Preference theory.

In a Fixprice model, on the other hand, the expectations (as we have formerly found) must be expectations of demand—of amount that will be demanded. The equilibrium stock (which now includes the less marketable assets) must be one which will fully satisfy expected demand (for any inability to satisfy demand involves loss of profit); and of those that do so it must be that which is expected to satisfy this demand at least cost.

It is common to say (and one easily falls into saying) that the equilibrium stock is that which is adjusted to *current* demand; this, indeed, is pretty much what Marshall said. But in general it is by no means adequate to say this. For the capital stock which is appropriate to a demand which is constant at its current level is one thing; the stock which is appropriate to a demand which is increasing from its present level at a certain growth rate will ordinarily be quite different. It can be a source of great confusion if this distinction is not borne in mind. We must, in general, be prepared to think of the equilibrium stock in the broader way.

The point has come when we must turn to the other side. What of 'flow equilibrium'? We are accustomed, working in terms of Marshallian theory, to think of flow equilibrium as something rather simple; and this notion did not have to be disturbed so long as we were dealing with a perishable product. But in general things are by no means so simple. The flow aspect of equilibrium is treacherous in the extreme.

Let us try to pass from the concept of stock equilibrium, as we have been defining it, into period analysis. If a unit is in stock equilibrium at the beginning of the period, and is still in stock equilibrium at the end, we shall want to say that it is in flow equilibrium during the period. There is no harm in that; but do we gain anything from it? Will it not be better, and more in accordance with our former terminology,[3] to say that it is in equilibrium over time *during the period*? It is in equilibrium over time if there is both stock equilibrium and flow equilibrium; but is that a helpful statement? Should we not just say that equilibrium over time requires a maintenance of stock equilibrium—which is all that needs to be said?

Even so, there are qualifications. For now that we have two stock equilibria to take account of (or to contend with) we have to consider whether the assumptions under which these stock equilibria are constructed (in particular, the expectations on which they are based) are consistent with one another. It would be wrong to say that a unit was in equilibrium over time during the period if it was in stock equilibrium at the beginning, and in stock equilibrium at the end, but these equilibria were based upon different expectations, so that the end-stock equilibrium came about, as it were, by accident. There is no difficulty about this if we restrict ourselves to taking flow equilibrium *ex ante*; if we say that the unit is in flow equilibrium if it is in stock equilibrium at the beginning, and *expects* to be in stock equilibrium at the end. But this, though useful in its way, is hardly sufficient.

We can cut the knot if we recall the convention, which we have used on other occasions, that the single period is such that changes in expectations do not occur within it; they only occur at the junction from one single period to the next. The *end* of the one period is then to be distinguished from the beginning of the next by the change in expectations which may occur when this same instant of time 'puts on its other hat'. It will follow that in each single period, taken by itself, expectations (of demand in later periods) will remain unchanged; so the end-stock can be compared with the beginning-stock in a consistent manner. We can then stick to the statement that there is flow equilibrium when there is stock equilibrium at the beginning of the single period, and there is also stock equilibrium at the end. This flow equilibrium is also equilibrium over time during the period; there does not, so far, seem to be any adequate reason to distinguish.

There is nevertheless one reason why we need some sort of a distinction. Even though we insist upon defining flow equilibrium as a *maintenance* of stock equilibrium, additional conditions are necessary, together with the stock equilibrium conditions, in order that stock

---

[3] See above, pp. 20–1.

equilibrium should be maintained. These conditions are quite properly described as *conditions of flow equilibrium*. But they are necessary, not sufficient conditions. If they are satisfied, in addition to the stock conditions, there is (we may now safely say) equilibrium over time. But if they are satisfied, while the stock conditions are not satisfied, it seems doubtful whether the resulting situation should be described as one of equilibrium at all.

Let us now proceed to test these definitions by considering some examples—first of all, our familiar examples.

The stationary economy is in equilibrium over time, we may now say, because it is in stock equilibrium (the same stock equilibrium) at every point of time. Expectations are stationary, and the stock conditions indicate that balance-sheets are adjusted to these stationary expectations. The flow conditions (that production equals consumption, or—better—that current demands are equal to new outputs) ensure that stock equilibrium can be maintained. In this simplest of all cases, that is all that there is to be said.

The regularly progressive economy, as always, has much more to it. It also, we may now say, is in equilibrium over time—because it is in stock equilibrium throughout. But its stock equilibrium, at the beginning and end of each single period, will not be the same. For now it is expected that demand will be continuing to expand (at a constant rate). Expected demand will therefore be greater at the end of a period than it was at the beginning. (The demand that is now expected t periods hence will be what was then demanded $t + 1$ periods hence; which is greater than what was then demanded t periods hence.) The capital stock must be expanded to be appropriate to this increased demand, if stock equilibrium is to be maintained. There can be no equilibrium over time unless there is this expansion of the capital stock. Flow conditions will therefore include the condition that production should just cover consumption demand plus this required investment: $cg = s$. The Harrod condition emerges as a flow condition of equilibrium over time, in the regularly progressive case. It is then a necessary condition, in order that stock equilibrium should be maintained.

Even the regularly progressive economy is a simplified case; our definitions should have a wider scope. It is not necessary that demand expectations should have either of the simple forms so far discussed. More complex cases will soon become very complex; but it is necessary to peer at them a little in order to understand more fully what it is that we have been doing.

Let us suppose—just to get a manageable example—that consumption demand is expected to remain stationary for so many periods, and after that to increase at a given (constant) rate. At the end of the current period the up-turn will have come one period nearer; end-stock equilibrium will thus require a larger capital than beginning-stock equilibrium; the flow conditions will accordingly entail some positive investment, and hence some positive saving, even in the current period, in which consumption demand is not expanding. Under this condition the economy can be in equilibrium over time, with its capital continually adjusted (as well as it can be adjusted) to these (perhaps anomalous) expectations. And so on for similar cases.

A word should perhaps be added on a question that may have been troubling the reader: is the use that we have just been making of the concept of equilibrium over time consistent with our earlier usage? We have here been taking expectations as given, and have been confining equilibrium over time *during the period* to an organization of the economy (both stock and flow) that is consistent with those given expectations. Should we not proceed the other way? Should we not say that an economy is in equilibrium over time if (and only if) expectations are *right*: if the expectations on which plans are based yield consistent plans—plans that can be carried through? This was a line of thought that arose naturally out of Temporary Equilibrium theory. There (as shown)[4] we do come naturally to a concept of long-period equilibrium over time, of which the accordance of expectation with realization is the distinguishing mark. What we say here must be kept in line with it.

The equilibrium over time that we have been discussing in this chapter is an equilibrium of the single period. If the single period is to have no more than a short duration (as we have usually implied to be the case) it can only be a short-period equilibrium over time. There is no reason why the period over which the equilibrium over time extends should not sometimes be short, sometimes long. We can get a long-period equilibrium over time by stringing several short equilibria together.

Even the longest period must be taken to have an end. Appropriate organization during the period must still depend upon the stock that

[4] p. 78.

is to be left at the end of the period. If there is to be equilibrium over time, even over a long period, there must be an end-stock equilibrium which is governed by expectations of what is to come afterwards. Such expectations must, in some sense, be data: they cannot be determined as consequences of what goes on within the period. This is true whether we are working with a Fixprice or with a Flexprice model. Something must always be assumed about the further future; in that sense there must always be some residual expectations that must be taken as exogenous.

I have said that equilibrium over time requires the maintenance of stock equilibrium. This may be interpreted as meaning that there is stock equilibrium, not only at the beginning and at the end of the period, but throughout its course. Thus, when we regard a 'long' period as a sequence of 'short' periods, the 'long' period can only be in equilibrium over time if every 'short' period in it is in equilibrium over time. Since expectations are to be kept self-consistent, there can be no revision of expectations at the junction between one 'short' period and its successor. The system is in stock equilibrium at each of these junctions; and is in stock equilibrium with respect to these consistent expectations. That can only be possible if expectations—with respect to demands that accrue within the 'long' period—are right. Equilibrium over time does imply consistency between expectations and realizations within the period; it is only the expectations of the further future that are arbitrary—as they must be.

So much for stock equilibrium—and for flow equilibrium. It has taken us much trouble to get them right: trouble which the reader may have felt that they hardly deserved, for in Fixprice theory (our main concern) they are little more than bench-marks or standards of reference. What bearing does all this have upon disequilibrium? The main point that has emerged is negative; but it is a negative point of much importance.

If we start from a condition in which there is stock equilibrium (for the 'unit', such as a firm, or for the economy) flow equilibrium conditions ensure its maintenance; but what happens in the more important case when we do not start from stock equilibrium? Flow equilibrium conditions can still be written down (or can usually be written down), but what is their significance? All that they can determine (if they are sufficient to determine it) is the path that the economy would follow if it began with a capital stock that was appropriate to a position upon that path. In that sense the path that is determined is an *equilibrium path*. But if the initial position is not one of stock equilibrium it is not the path that will be followed, nor can we assume that there will be any tendency for it to be approached. It is, at the best, the 'long-period equilibrium' of the system; but whether there is any tendency for that long-period equilibrium to be approached, if we do not start from a position upon its path, is a question that must be left, for the present, entirely open.

10

A PROBLEM IN STOCK ADJUSTMENT

It will probably assist understanding of the distinctions which have been drawn in the preceding chapter if we see in detail how they work out in a simple case. I shall pursue this simple case rather far, and (as will be seen) the further working out of it is by no means simple. I am not suggesting that this working out is of more than illustrative importance. When the reader has had enough of it he will doubtless pass on. But some sort of illustration, at this point, does seem to be required.

The problem which I shall take is entirely 'micro'. It solely concerns the behaviour of the individual producer (or stock-holder). And it solely concerns that part of his behaviour which relates to the stock (or inventory) of finished product. In particular, the whole question of investment in fixed capital is left entirely on one side.

Prices being fixed, the state of demand is given from outside—it is an exogenous variable. The backwash of changes in production on demand (the multiplier effects which are so important in macro-analysis) is entirely neglected.

––––––––––

Let us suppose that our single producer has a single (storable) product, that takes n periods to produce. A decision about the amount to produce, or rather to begin producing, can be taken, according to our usual convention, once a period. (It does not matter whether the process of production is or is not carried on in the same firm as that in which the stocks are held. If it is in a different firm, then the assumption is that orders take n periods to execute.) These assumptions give a convenient framework within which to operate; I do not think that they are unduly restrictive.

As a preliminary, consider what happens when there is a once-for-all increase in demand. We then begin (as is commonly done) from a state of stationary equilibrium in this particular market. If it were certain that demand would remain stationary, no stock (or inventory) would be required. We may, however, admit some degree of uncertainty, so that even in stationary equilibrium there should be some positive stock, related in some manner to the level of demand. The stock-equilibrium condition (the only stock-equilibrium condition which is here of significance) is that the actual stock should equal this desired stock. The flow-equilibrium condition is that current output should equal current demand, so that the producer can *remain* in stock equilibrium. These two conditions being satisfied, there is equilibrium over time (as far as our particular producer is concerned).

Now suppose that there supervenes a significant rise in demand (an unexpected rise), after which demand remains constant at the new level. During the time that elapses before increased output can be ready, there *must* be a fall in stock—an increasing degree of stock disequilibrium. But it is by no means necessary that increased production should be started as soon as the increase in demand shows itself; some time may have to elapse before it is clear that what has occurred is a permanent rise, not a mere random variation. The longer this delay, the larger will be the fall in stock. But even when production is increased, if it is only increased enough to restore the flow condition of equilibrium (so that production again becomes equal to demand when the new output is ready), full equilibrium will not be restored. The state will still be one of stock disequilibrium; all that will have happened, by the adjustment that has so far occurred, is that the stock disequilibrium will be prevented from getting worse. Stock equilibrium will only be restored when the stock has been rebuilt; after there has been an additional (temporary) increase in output to replenish the depleted stock.

This is a situation which continually arises in practice; and in so simple a case as this the producer would certainly have no difficulty in making his adjustment. Knowing how long production takes, and how long he has himself delayed before taking action, he has only to decide in how much of a hurry he is, and so whether to spread the temporary expansion over a shorter or longer time, and his task is done. More generally, indeed, it is by no means so simple. The adjustment of stock to a fluctuating demand will need quite a bit of steering. There is always the double problem: on the one hand he must estimate what the future course of demand will be, and on the other he must correct the excesses and deficiencies of stock that result from past mistakes. Neither of these is an easy problem to solve; but they are nevertheless problems that are solved, more or less well, in the ordinary course of business management.

It is the second of these problems on which I am concentrating in this chapter. It would be immensely convenient, for the purpose of economic analysis, if we could find some way of representing a reasonable reaction to stock disequilibrium by a *rule* of conduct. We could then incorporate that rule into our models; this would enable us to calculate not merely the equilibrium path of the model, but something which might prove to be a good representation of the actual path which (under the conditions proposed) would be likely to be followed. The cycle models which have been constructed by economists[1] do generally incorporate (more or less explicitly) some such rule. But when one tries out these rules, even on so simple a 'micro' problem as that with which we are at present concerned, they do not seem to give good results. By deliberate steering, the ordinary business should usually be able to do better than it appears to do in such a mechanical model. The mechanical models are certainly suggestive, but it is not clear that we are wise to take them as anything more than that.

In order to show this I need some notation. Let D_t be the demand, O_t the output, of period t. Let I_t be production *started* in period t, so that $O_t = I_{t-n}$ (for production takes n periods). Let S_t be the actual stock, S_t^* the desired stock, at the *beginning* of period t. It is clearly necessary that

$$S_{t+1} - S_t = O_t - D_t.$$

I shall write

$$S_t^* - S_t = E_t$$

so that in stock equilibrium $E_t = 0$.

(1) The first rule to be considered is the 'Stock Adjustment Principle',[2] according to which the production started in any period is equal to a flow component F (based on what demand is expected to be when the output is ready) plus some fraction of the deficiency E. That is to say,

$$I_t = F_t + \lambda E_t$$

whence

$$O_t = I_{t-n} = F_{t-n} + \lambda E_{t-n}$$

$$S_{t+1} - S_t = F_{t-n} - D_t + \lambda E_{t-n}$$

[1] By myself and by many others.

[2] I borrow this term from R. C. O. Matthews (*The Trade Cycle*, p. 49). As Matthews observes, the Acceleration Principle, as commonly understood, is a special case of this more general principle.

$$E_{t+1} - E_t = (S^*_{t+1} - S^*_t) - (F_{t-n} - D_t + \lambda E_{t-n})$$

or
$$E_{t+1} - E_t + \lambda E_{t-n} = S^*_{t+1} - S^*_t + D_t - F_{t-n},$$

the *fundamental difference equation* of this method of adjustment.

If equilibrium were maintained throughout, the left-hand side of this fundamental equation would be zero; the right-hand side must therefore be zero. Now all the components of the right-hand side depend in some way upon the manner in which demand (D) moves over time. Corresponding to any given movement of demand, there will be certain movements of F and S^* which will maintain equilibrium. If, for instance, demand was completely stationary, equilibrium would be maintained if S^* were stationary (so that $S^*_{t+1} = S^*_t$), and if production started were always equal to demand ($F_{t-n} = D_t$). If demand was expanding at a constant rate, and S^* was expanding with it, F_{t-n} would have to exceed D_t by an amount sufficient to supply this *equilibrium* increase in stock—so that the increase in demand would have to be foreseen accurately, and the equilibrium increase in stock would also have to be provided for. And so on, if demand were varying in other (foreseen) manners.

Thus if the firm were in equilibrium in time, the right-hand side of our fundamental equation would be zero; but the vanishing of the right-hand side is not a sufficient condition of equilibrium; it is simply what we have been calling the flow condition. If (as in our elementary case of a once-for-all increase in demand) there is a disturbance of equilibrium, there will be initial (disequilibrium) positions in which the E's will not be zero; afterwards, when demand has settled down on to its new path, the right-hand side should again be zero, so that we must have

$$E_{t+1} - E_t + \lambda E_{t-n} = 0$$

though the individual E's are not necessarily zero. This is a difference equation in the E's, the solution of which must depend upon n (the period of production) and upon λ, and upon them only. We can examine whether the 'Stock Adjustment Principle' (as defined) will lead back to equilibrium (or on to the equilibrium path) by asking whether this difference equation, starting from arbitrary values of the E's, will converge to a zero solution.

This is a purely mathematical question which can be explored by the methods that I have described elsewhere.[3] The equation is more

---

[3] *Contribution to the Theory of the Trade Cycle*, Appendix, esp. pp. 187 ff.

difficult than that which gives the 'elementary case' of Accelerator theory, but it turns out to have very similar properties. There are two critical values of λ, which we may call λ_1 and λ_2. If $0 < \lambda < \lambda_1$, there will be a straightforward convergence to equilibrium, without any fluctuations save those that arise as a consequence of the arbitrary initial values. If $\lambda_1 < \lambda < \lambda_2$, there will be damped fluctuations. If $\lambda > \lambda_2$, the fluctuations will be explosive.

Mathematical formulae for λ_1 and λ_2 can be worked out;[4] their general significance can, however, be explained in simpler terms.

It is obvious that if $\lambda = 1$, while $n > 1$, far too much new production would be started. Enough processes would be started in each single period to fill the whole gap between actual and desired stock that existed in that period; there would thus be a whole series of new startings, one after another, all effectively directed at filling the same gap. That is nonsense; a sensible value of λ must be far smaller than that. A value which naturally suggests itself is $(1/n)$; for 'induced investment', repeated at this rate, would just suffice to close the gap over the whole period of production. But even that, it is not surprising to discover, is too much. For if $\lambda = (1/n)$ is applied to the example with which we began, of the single increase in demand which runs down inventories during the period of production, it becomes apparent that the same fall in inventories is corrected more than once. In fact, it turns out that $\lambda = (1/n)$ gives a fluctuating solution, which is indeed damped, but not very heavily damped. We get a good idea of the values of λ_1 and λ_2 if we take them as

$$\lambda_1 = (1/3)(1/n), \quad \lambda_2 = (3/2)(1/n)$$

so that $\lambda = (1/n)$ lies between the two critical values, but much nearer to the second than to the first.[5]

I conclude that if, on this principle, there is to be a smooth convergence to equilibrium, the induced investment must be spread very thinly; and (of course) if it is spread very thinly, it will take a long time before equilibrium is restored.

(2) This being so, it is natural to ask whether we could not get a better result from a different rule. The tendency to fluctuation (or rather the *kind* of fluctuation) which we have found to result from the

---

[4] They were stated, and proved, in Appendix A to *Capital and Growth* (1965); it does not seem worth while to reproduce this here.

[5] If n is large, λ_1 tends to e^{-1} $(1/n)$, and λ_2 to $(\pi/2)$ $(1/n)$; the approximation to values close to these, even for small n, is rather surprisingly fast. (It is easily seen that if $n = 1$, $\lambda_1 = \frac{1}{4}$, $\lambda_2 = 1$.)

Stock Adjustment Principle, was basically due to the translation of a stock condition into a flow condition: the *flow* of induced investment being made dependent upon the *state* of stock. It might be thought that this could be avoided, if induced investment were made to depend upon *changes* in stock: or, more strictly, on changes in E, the excess of desired stock over actual. It would be a plausible ingredient in a stock policy to suppose that replacement would be stepped up when E was rising, and vice versa.

If this were the only factor affecting the induced investment, we should find (on working through the analysis) that the λE_{t-n} of the former equation was replaced by a difference term, so that the critical difference equation took the form

$$E_{t+1} - E_t + \lambda (E_{t-n} - E_{t-n-1}) = 0$$

and this is an equation which is very easily solved. For it simply means that $E_{t+1} - E_t$ is $(-\lambda)$ of what it was $(n+1)$ periods before. Thus if $\lambda < 1$ (as we may again, but perhaps not so confidently, suppose) $E_{t+1} - E_t$ must converge to zero, though (in view of the negative sign of the multiplier) only after fluctuations. Even so, this does not mean that E_t will converge to zero; it only means that E_t will converge to a constant value (a constant that will depend upon initial conditions). There is no convergence to equilibrium, only to a constant degree of disequilibrium. As a rule that is to be taken by itself, this rule is even less attractive than its predecessor.

There is, however, of course no reason why it should be taken by itself. A producer might quite possibly work mainly on the Stock Adjustment Principle, but might also be influenced to some extent by the way in which his E was rising or falling. (One would indeed think that this would be a very natural thing to happen.) The tendencies to fluctuation which are due to the two components would then be superposed. In superposition they might offset one another, but there does not seem to be any general reason why they should do so. It is difficult to give a mathematical demonstration; one would, however, guess that they would be more likely to reinforce one another.

(3) There is still another rule which deserves investigation. The defect in the 'Stock Adjustment Principle', as we have so far taken it, is that (as has been explained) it sets the producer filling what is essentially the same gap more than once. (This defect is of course not noticeable if, as is common in trade cycle models, decisions are only supposed to be taken once in every period of production—if the period

of production and the decision period are taken to be the same. But as soon as we distinguish the two periods—and surely we ought to distinguish them—we have to face up to it.)

Now it may fairly be maintained that businesses do not in practice make this fault, because they know that the production which is designed to fill the gap is already in the pipeline. We have left that knowledge out of account, but in practice it is bound to be taken into account. It could formally be taken into account if the Stock Adjustment Principle were *enlarged*; if it were applied, not simply (as we have so far applied it) to the inventory of finished product, but to the whole of the circulating capital—inventory *plus* goods in process.

This enlarged rule could formally be worked out in the same way as the other; but as soon as we make the attempt we run into a difficulty. How do we value the goods in process? They would of course be valued in practice in terms of the labour and materials that had been put into them at each stage, a profit to cover overheads not being added until sale (so that it has nothing to do with the *relative* values of goods in process and final inventory). Now there is no reason why these labour and materials should be applied at a constant rate; all sorts of patterns of time application are possible. The proportion of the total prime cost that will be attributed to the unfinished product, when a given fraction of its total production time has elapsed, may thus vary quite considerably for this purely technical reason. But such differences have nothing to do with the question that here concerns us. It is entirely possible that there might be one productive process, with one time-shape of application, where the use of the enlarged rule made for an easy convergence to equilibrium, while there was another, with a different time weighting, where it did not. Thus it looks unlikely that we can give a general verdict on the enlarged principle. The best that we can hope to do is to work out special cases.

One special case which looks as if it would deserve discussion is the 'point-input' case, in which the whole value is put into the article as soon as it is started, so that goods in process are valued as equivalent to finished products. Though this is not a realistic assumption, it puts the maximum possible weight upon the 'goods in process' component, so that it should be the limiting case, at the other extreme from that which we began by examining (when no weight at all was placed upon them). Let us see how this case would come out, if we submitted it to the same analysis as we did the other.

The enlarged Stock Adjustment Principle may still be expressed as $I_t = F_t + \lambda E_t$, where F_t is the same flow component, but E_t, the excess of desired over actual, is now to relate to the *whole circulating capital*. That is to say, $E_t = K_t^* - K_t$, where $K_t = S_t + C_t$, in which S_t (as before) is the inventory, while C_t is goods in process. Our *special* 'point-input' assumption will now be expressed by putting:

$$C_t = I_{t-1} + I_{t-2} + \ldots + I_{t-n+1}$$

(on any other assumption about time-shape the Is would have weights that were less than 1, increasing from left to right).

Thus $E_t = K_t^* - (S_t + I_{t-1} + I_{t-2} + \ldots I_{t-n+1})$.

As before $S_{t+1} - S_t = O_t - D_t = I_{t-n} - D_t$

and so

$$
\begin{aligned}
E_{t+1} - E_t &= K_{t+1}^* - K_t^* - (S_{t+1} - S_t) - (I_t - I_{t-n+1}) \\
&= K_{t+1}^* - K_t^* - (I_{t-n} - D_t) - (I_t - I_{t-n+1}) \\
&= K_{t+1}^* - K_t^* + D_t - F_{t-n} - F_t + F_{t-n+1} - \\
&\qquad\qquad\qquad\qquad - \lambda(E_{t-n} + E_t - E_{t-n+1}),
\end{aligned}
$$

an equation which is now in a form which is suitable for the same treatment as we gave to the corresponding equation in the 'unenlarged' case.

Putting all Es = 0, we get the flow condition; then, supposing the flow condition of equilibrium to be already established, we get the critical difference equation

$$E_{t+1} - (1 - \lambda)E_t - \lambda(E_{t-n+1} - E_{t-n}) = 0.$$

The effectiveness for equilibration of the enlarged Stock Adjustment Principle (on our particular assumption about time-shape of inputs) can then be tested, as in the other case, by inquiring whether the sequence defined by this equation, if it starts from arbitrary Es, will converge to $E = 0$.

From an analysis of this equation the following conclusions appear to follow.[6]

It should first be noticed that if $n = 1$, this equation is the same as its predecessor; for (of course) if $n = 1$, 'enlargement' makes no difference. Accordingly, for $n = 1$, $\lambda_1 = (1/4)$, and $\lambda_2 = 1$, as before.

---

6 For this too, see Appendix A of *Capital and Growth*.

For any value of n greater than 1, either $\lambda_2 = (2/3)$ or it is so little above (2/3) as hardly to signify. This restriction is much less drastic than the corresponding restriction in the 'unenlarged' case, but that (of course) is as it should be. There ought now to be no question of filling the same gap more than once. Even so, the induced investment must be somewhat spread out if there is to be a convergence to equilibrium, even after fluctuations.

As for λ_1, it is larger than in the 'unenlarged' case, as we should expect, but it remains fairly small. It diminishes as n rises; for any value of n greater than 2, it is less than (1/6). The induced investment must still be very gentle indeed if there is to be no tendency for (even damped) fluctuation.

It is unnecessary to take this particular investigation any further; the reader may indeed feel that we have already taken it quite far enough. It is hardly a discovery to find that we are unable to 'simulate' the behaviour of intelligent business management by any simple rule. But I have thought it worth while to work the matter out in detail, for another reason. We needed an exercise in the working of the stock and flow analysis that was described in principle, but only in principle, in the preceding chapter. Instead of beginning with its application to the 'macro' problems, where it (or something like it) is most familiar, I thought it well to begin by trying it out on the 'micro' scale. We then keep close to the kind of thing which we can test out by our imagination—by putting ourselves in the position of the 'people' whose actions we are trying to represent. If we find—as we do find— that mechanical principles of adjustment do not offer a good representation, we shall have gained something in the way of scepticism about the use of such principles in more ambitious undertakings. And this (I think we shall find) will be quite useful to us later on.

11

KEYNES-TYPE MACRODYNAMICS

In this chapter, and in that which follows, I shall be considering the application of stock and flow analysis to Fixprice macroeconomics. Even within this limited field there are two kinds of model to be considered.

The first, with which in this chapter I shall be wholly concerned, is based upon that which was used by Keynes in the *General Theory*. It is not the same as the Keynes model (which, as I have repeatedly emphasized, is not strictly a dynamic model); but it has an unmistakable relation to the Keynes model, and it is by that relation that it is easiest to recognize and remember it.[1]

In Keynes, the volume of investment depends upon the rate of interest; it is read off from the 'marginal efficiency of capital' schedule. As soon as we interpret Keynes in a Fixprice sense (as many of his successors have been inclined to do), the rate of interest becomes an exogenous variable (like other prices), so that the *given* marginal efficiency of capital schedule becomes a *given* volume of investment. But to go so far as that, in a properly dynamic model, will be very inconvenient; if actual (*ex post*) investment is given, there is no room for a dynamic process to work. It is accordingly inevitable, when one is concerned with dynamic analysis, that the strict Keynes assumption should be relaxed in some way or other. It may be done by introducing lags, or by distinguishing between *ex ante* and *ex post* investment. I am going to suggest a rather different way, which leads to a form of analysis that seems to have a place in the present discussion.

Instead of supposing that the volume of investment, as a whole, is given exogenously, let us suppose that a part only is so given. Formally, it might be a large part or a small part. We might simply mark off some sort of 'long-range investment' as autonomous investment; or we might reckon as autonomous the whole of that investment

[1] I am tempted to follow the (undoubtedly appropriate) precedent of Professor Kahn who in his article on Duopoly (*Economic Journal*, 1938) used 'Cournotesque' in just the way that I have in mind. But 'Keynesesque' is too clumsy; 'Keynes-type' (like a 'claret-type' wine) will have to do.

which is the object of deliberate policy decisions, excluding only that part which takes place 'passively' (as a difference between *ex ante* and *ex post*). The choice which we make on this matter cannot be decided by an appeal to facts. It is not a question of fact; it is a question of what we are trying to do. One might use one classification for one purpose and one for another.[2]

The particular line which I shall use in this chapter will leave a big part of investment as autonomous—nothing less than the whole of investment in fixed capital. This is quite a convenient line in practical application. It is in fact the common practice of business to take decisions about investment in fixed capital in a different way, and on a different level, from decisions about investment in working capital and stocks—the former being a matter for the board of directors, the latter (since it is a resultant of innumerable day-to-day decisions) being only influenced indirectly by major decisions that are made 'at the top'. Thus the division at this line makes quite good sense. It is an interesting question to inquire into the working of an economy in which fixed capital investment is planned—along lines that are determined outside the model—while the rest of investment adjusts itself, as best it can, to that given pattern of autonomous fixed capital investment.

The initial stock of fixed capital, at the beginning of the process under consideration, must of course be assumed to be given; if *net* fixed capital investment in every capital good is also given, the size and composition of the fixed capital stock will be given throughout the whole of the process. It may, however, be maintained that it would be more sensible to take *gross* investment in fixed capital to be given autonomously, the extent of depreciation (or using-up) being left to be determined as a function of output as a whole. But if it is simply proportional to output as a whole there is no difficulty; I shall therefore simplify presentation by taking it that what is given is *net* fixed capital investment.

———

The working of a Keynes-type model, such as has been described, is mostly familiar; but it will be useful to set it down in the standard form to which we have been coming. One begins, of course, from the saving-investment *identity*. If A_t is net investment in fixed capital in period t, Y_t is income (or net output), and K_t is *working capital*

———

[2] In my *Trade Cycle* book I confined autonomous investment to the long-range variety; but it makes little difference to the formal argument whether a wide or a narrow definition is used.

(including stocks) at the commencement of period t, the identity can be written

$$A_t + (K_{t+1} - K_t) = sY_t$$

where s is the proportion of income saved. If, however, we write K_t^* for *desired* working capital, and $E_t = K_t^* - K_t$ (as in the previous chapter) the identity takes the form

$$A_t + (K^*_{t+1} - K_t^*) - sY_t = E_{t+1} - E_t$$

and a *flow condition of equilibrium* can be derived from it by setting E_{t+1} and E_t equal to zero.

Desired working capital must clearly depend upon the expected level of output; it should thus (in equilibrium) depend upon Y_t, Y_{t+1}, . . . , Y_{t+n}, where n is the number of periods that are taken by that process of production (starting from original factors, including fixed capital as an original factor) that takes longest. It is a simplification (though a very usual simplification) to make it depend upon Y_t alone. I shall, however, make use of this simplification, along with others, since it is irrelevant to the main points which I want to make.

Let us therefore put $K_t^* = cY_t$, so that c is a *working-capital*–output ratio. Our *flow condition of equilibrium* accordingly becomes

$$A_t + c(Y_{t+1} - Y_t) = sY_t$$

and this, it must be observed, is a *difference equation*. Even if c and s are taken to be constants, it will not, by itself, determine an equilibrium path. It is simply a rule by which, if Y_t is given, Y_{t+1} can be determined. Thus it only determines a particular equilibrium path if we are also supplied with an *initial condition*; for instance, if we are given a value for Y_0.

Once that initial value is provided, the difference equation will determine the *equilibrium* course of output, corresponding to *any* given movement of A_t. There is no need for us to assume that autonomous investment is increasing at a constant growth rate; it may follow any *given* path. It is indeed possible, with the simplifications that we have made, for the difference equation to be solved, rather easily, whatever the path of A_t. The general solution is

$$Y_t = \left(1 + \frac{s}{c}\right)^t Y_0 - \frac{1}{c}\left\{A_{t-1} + \left(1 + \frac{s}{c}\right)A_{t-2} + \ldots + \left(1 + \frac{s}{c}\right)^{t-1} A_0\right\}$$

Thus Y_t will always have a growth rate which is less than s/c; remembering that c is the *working* capital–output ratio, this makes good sense.

Let us look for a moment at the special case where autonomous investment has a constant growth rate g; so that $A_t = A_0 (1 + g)^t$. (Though this is a case that is easy to over-use, it has its uses as an important example.) The series in the square bracket then becomes a geometrical progression, and can be summed by the usual rule, giving

$$Y_t = \left(1 + \frac{s}{c}\right)^t \left(Y_0 - \frac{A_0}{s - cg}\right) + \frac{A_0}{s - cg} (1 + g)^t$$

In this case, then, equilibrium output has two components, one with the growth rate s/c, one with the growth rate g. Now it is clear that s/c must be greater than g. For if it were not so, though the first component would be positive, the second would be negative; and it would be this negative second component the size of which would be increasing faster. After a while, therefore, Y_t would certainly become negative —a possibility that must be ruled out. With constantly increasing (positive) autonomous investment, equilibrium output cannot be allowed to behave so badly. The condition $s > cg$ in fact says no more than that there is enough saving to support the increase in fixed capital and the consequential increase in working capital.

If $s > cg$, the second component is necessarily positive; but now it is the first component which has the faster rate of growth. Accordingly, if $Y_0 < A_0/(s - cg)$, we shall again find that Y_t becomes negative for large t. It follows that we cannot impose *any* initial Y_0 and get a sensible sequence for Y_t. We must have either Y_0 greater than or equal to $A_0/(s - cg)$.

In the former case, both components in Y_t will be positive, but the first will be growing faster. The growth rate of Y_t will therefore be rising towards the growth rate of this first component, which is s/c. But if investment in fixed capital is growing at a growth rate g, the total stock of fixed capital (though its initial growth rate may be in excess of g) must ultimately tend to rise at a growth rate g. Output will then be trying to rise at a growth rate s/c, which is larger than g. There must therefore, sooner or later, be a shortage of fixed capital. If there is not to be a shortage, the growth rate of Y_t must not be larger than g. And this can only happen (we now see) if $Y_0 = A_0/(s - cg)$, so that $Y_t = Y_0(1 + g)^t$.

Thus there is, after all, only one equilibrium path of output—in this particular case.

What has happened? In the light of our general principles about stock and flow conditions it is not hard to locate the trouble. As I have repeatedly insisted, the flow condition is not a sufficient condition of equilibrium; thus it is not surprising to find that the equilibrium path cannot be adequately identified by mere manipulation of the flow condition. In order to determine the equilibrium path, stock conditions as well as flow conditions must be considered.

It may nevertheless be objected: have we not already made use of the stock condition? We have already taken it that desired capital (K_t^*) depends upon expected output (Y_t on our simplification). Surely this is a stock condition: yet it appears that it does not do its job. The answer, I think we must conclude, is that this condition is not the only stock condition. Though we have assumed that investment in fixed capital is given autonomously, it remains true that its holding of fixed assets is a part of the balance-sheet of the representative firm; a balance between holdings of fixed capital assets and of working capital assets is still to be required, as a necessary element in stock (or balance-sheet) equilibrium. The holding of fixed capital assets is, by assumption, a given magnitude, at each stage of the process; but the holding of working capital assets is a variable, which must nevertheless bear a certain relation to the holding of fixed capital assets, if equilibrium is to be maintained. One may indeed not wish to press this proportionality too exactly; for the ratio is not one that firms may be expected, in practice, to watch very closely. But, as is already apparent from our study of the particular case of the constant autonomous investment growth rate, any significant departure from a normal ratio is likely to build up. What began as a tolerable discrepancy builds up into something that is quite intolerable. I therefore conclude that proportionality (or approximate proportionality) between investment in working capital and in fixed capital is a condition that we ought to impose, when we are seeking to determine the Equilibrium Path of a Keynes-type model.

With this additional condition everything becomes very simple. The flow condition of equilibrium is just the saving-investment equation, with the whole of investment (in equilibrium) deducible from autonomous investment, so that Y_t (in equilibrium) is then deducible from the saving propensity (just the old multiplier). The Keynes-type model reduces to the familiar form, after all.

But, from all that has so far been said, all we have got is the equilibrium path. It is an equilibrium path (it must be insisted) only in the sense that *if* the initial stock of working capital is appropriate, and *if* demand-expectations are right, it is the path that will be followed. Nothing has been said about any tendency towards this equilibrium—from a disequilibrium position. It is the common practice, in Keynesian Economics, to take it for granted that there will be a rapid movement to equilibrium; so that the equilibrium position of an economy can be taken to represent its actual position, to be at least a fair approximation to it. But it will not be supposed, after our discussion of the corresponding micro-problem in the preceding chapter, that we shall be able to make any confident statement about a tendency to the equilibrium that has been here described.[3]

Let us proceed in the conventional manner with an equilibrium motion that is *disturbed*. That is to say, we start with an economy that is in equilibrium with respect to a given path of autonomous investment; expectations are right, and the stocks of working capital are such as to be appropriate to this particular path. We need not assume (any more than we did in Chapter 10) that the stocks are no more than are technologically necessary to support this growth path; the stocks that are necessary to permit a 'normal' degree of flexibility may also be supposed to be carried. Then, in a particular period, there is a shift in autonomous investment. It increases (we will first suppose) beyond what it was expected in the past to be for the current period. It is *possible* that there can be an immediate (or nearly immediate) adjustment to a new equilibrium, that which corresponds to the new autonomous investment path?

I will begin by constructing a case in which it is possible that there could be a very direct adjustment. Suppose that production (both of fixed capital goods and of consumption goods) takes place in a series of stages, of equal length, each stage using the product of the preceding as raw material. Say that each stage lasts one month. Then, if there is an unforeseen spurt in autonomous investment—more new

---

[3] It may perhaps have been noticed by some readers that in the last two sections I have been trying to mend a hole (of which I have for years been conscious) in the argument of my book on the *Trade Cycle*. The Equilibrium Path (as it appears, for example, in the diagram on p. 97 of that book) has long seemed to me to be inadequately defined. Even in the mathematical treatment (pp. 174–6 and 197–8 of the Appendix) it only appears as the limit to which the 'actual' process will converge, if it converges; but what if (as I frequently wanted to suppose) it does not converge? I still wanted to have an equilibrium path, if only for purposes of reference. I am now convinced that the trouble arose from inadequate attention to stock conditions; this is what I am now trying to explain.

production of fixed capital goods is started in a particular month than was expected—there will be a direct increase in the employment of labour in that month (on the new fixed capital good production), and a consequential increase in demand for consumption goods, which we shall suppose to take place within the same month (there is no consumption lag). During the month that increased demand for consumption goods can only be met out of stocks; and it can be so met, if it is not too large, for we are taking it for granted that there are 'normal' stocks of consumption goods that can be run down.

Now it is just conceivable that at the moment when the additional consumption demand appears, production in the final stage should be increased. The deficiency in stocks of consumption goods might then be remedied within the month, so that, at the end of the month, the stock of the final product would already have reached its new equilibrium. But in order for this to be, even technically, possible, there must have been a stock of the raw material of the final stage; otherwise the production of the final stage could not have been stepped up. We may suppose (in accordance with our 'normal stock' hypothesis) that this stock does exist. But then, if final stage production is stepped up, and nothing else happens, the fall in stocks is simply passed one stage further back. Again, however, it is just conceivable (though with even more difficulty) that as soon as the increase in demand for the product of the penultimate stage began to declare itself, production in that stage also would be stepped up; but for this to be possible there must again be a stock of the raw material of the penultimate stage on which that stage can work. And so on, right back to the beginning.[4]

It seems to follow that if production is divided into equal stages, and if response to a change in demand is immediate all along the line, it is possible that stock equilibrium may be restored at the end of the 'month'. From that point onwards there is of course no difficulty. Accordingly, if we take the single period to be one month, and if these conditions are satisfied, the system is again in equilibrium at the end of the single period.

But it is only too obvious what drastic assumptions we have to make in order that this should be possible. The necessary reaction is

---

[4] If there is a beginning. It is not unrealistic to suppose that there is; we can have a first stage in which there is no raw material, since we are assuming that there is a given stock of fixed capital, which may include land. The first stage may be extractive. But I do not think that this is essential to the argument.

(as I have said elsewhere[5]) 'unbelievably quick'. But even that is not enough. It is also necessary that stocks should be held at regular intervals in the production process; and it will ordinarily be impossible technologically that they should be so held. It is of course always possible to divide a production process, arbitrarily, into equal-length stages; but some (perhaps many) of them will then be stages at which it is technologically impossible to hold stocks. It will then be impossible that equilibrium should be restored, after a disturbance, until quite a long interval has elapsed. And this is apart from the question of lags in adjustment. If there is a lag, the time taken for adjustment must be even longer.

It is in fact unreasonable to suppose that there will not be a lag. Accordingly, in the first period after autonomous investment has increased, there will be a fall in stocks, either entirely at the final stage of consumption goods production, or (in part) at earlier stages. At this point the rise in autonomous investment is partially offset by a fall in working capital (induced) investment, so that total output (Y) rises only to something short of its new equilibrium level. But so long as actual output remains, in this manner, below its equilibrium path, stocks will be falling, and ever more falling, below their equilibrium level; sooner or later this gap must be made up. As soon as an attempt is made to fill this gap, output will rise relatively to its equilibrium path, and will then rise above the equilibrium path, remaining above it until the gap has been filled.

Now, it is tempting to treat this 'spurt' or 'hump' in induced investment as if it were wholly analogous to the original rise in autonomous investment, so that it will lead to consequences of a similar character. It is certainly true that it also involves a rise in inputs, with a consequent effect upon the demand for finished products; it will therefore induce a 'multiplier' expansion of its own, on the top of that engendered by the original expansion (the expansion of output that was incorporated in the equilibrium path). But, especially in view of what we have learned (in the preceding chapter) about the corresponding disequilibrium on the micro-level, it would seem unwise to be dogmatic about the form which this secondary expansion *must* take. In particular, it would be unwise to assume that it must take the form which can be deduced by mechanical application of an 'Accelerator' or 'Stock Adjustment Principle'.

[5] *Trade Cycle*, p. 50.

This is not to say that calculation of the cyclical movements, which emerge when we 'turn the handle' according to such rules, is a pure waste of time. It does unquestionably have an illustrative value; it is a useful indicator of the kind of thing that can happen. But one should not put too much weight upon it.[6] There is a most important distinction between the induced investment which is allowed for in the determination of the equilibrium path, and that which arises in the process of equilibration. The former is a technical necessity; it arises out of permanent factors in the technique of production, such as are expressible in a capital–output ratio. The latter is much more 'psychological' in character. It depends, first of all, on the amount of initial divergence from the equilibrium path; and this, though (as we have seen) it is partly a matter of technology, is mainly a matter of the way the change in demand is interpreted, of the way it is read, of the expectations which it engenders. As soon as there is a gap—as soon as actual stock falls, significantly, below desired stock—the deficiency must somehow, sooner or later, be made up. But how quickly it has to be made up depends upon the degree of discomfort which businesses experience when they are out of stock equilibrium; and that is a thing which has been left quite undetermined by the things that have been taken into account in the model under discussion.

It is not surprising, in the light of the foregoing, to find that simple Accelerator formulae rarely provide a good fit to the time-shape of actual cycles. The forces which the formulae take into account may still be the main forces at work; but the things which determine the time-shape of the cycles which they produce are of a more complex character.

If, still starting from an equilibrium position, one had worked out the effects of a downward (instead of an upward) shift in autonomous investment, most of the preceding analysis could have been put, without qualification, into reverse. There is more possibility of interrupting in the middle a process that has been begun than of starting in the middle a process that has not been begun; but the loss involved in such interruption is usually severe, so that it will not occur unless prospects are rather desperate. In all but such extreme cases, we must expect that there will be some unwanted accumulation of stocks, as a result of the initial downward shift—some necessary accumulation,

---

[6] Work upon the periods of the cycles that are generated by such mechanisms is (I have now come to think) particularly a waste of time.

but an actual accumulation that goes beyond what is technologically necessary. There will then be a surplus that has to be worked off— sooner or later, quickly or slowly.

What, however, if (as will surely be the case in application) we do not start from an equilibrium position? If, initially, the stock of working capital is too large, relative to its equilibrium amount, the excess will be due to be worked off, with the consequences with which we are now familiar. A fall in autonomous investment, below what was expected, if it occurred in that case, would have an additive effect; but a rise in autonomous investment would diminish the surplus, so that a movement into equilibrium would be easier than it was before. Similarly if the initial disequilibrium was the other way. These (of course) were the situations with which Keynes (writing when he did) was most immediately concerned; but the others, that are more likely to give rise to inventory cycles, would deserve, in a truly 'general' theory, at least equal attention.[7]

[7] I have set out a simple version of multiplier theory, which takes account of the complications that have been more formally considered in this chapter, in the chapter on the multiplier in *Crisis in Keynesian Economics* (1974).

12

HARROD-TYPE MACRODYNAMICS

The Keynes-type theory, if it is formulated in the way that we have been formulating it, obviously needs to be completed by a consideration of what happens when fixed capital investment is not given autonomously, but is itself dependent, in whole or in part, on changes in output. I am still inclined to believe that there are purposes for which it is wise to leave a part of fixed capital investment autonomous (as I did in my *Trade Cycle* book); if one is thinking of a model that is to throw light on actual historical experience, it is as well that there should be a part of the phenomena which one's model does not attempt to explain. But for purposes of pure theory, where our object is the understanding of the principles on which economic processes work, it may be better to be more extreme. The working of an economy in which all investment is induced investment, is one of the things which we should like to understand. It is a model of this kind which I shall call a Harrod-type model.[1]

The basic algebra of such a model is very familiar, but we had better write it out, in our terms. Prices, as usual, are taken to be fixed, and there is no shortage of labour. Let K_t (now) be the whole stock of capital at the commencement of period t (fixed capital as well as working capital being included). Then the saving-investment identity is merely

$$K_{t+1} - K_t = sY_t$$

without any autonomous term. If the desired capital (K_t^*) bears a constant proportion (c) to output (Y_t), then, in equilibrium (where $K_t = K_t^*$ and $K_{t+1} = K_{t+1}^*$)

$$c(Y_{t+1} - Y_t) = sY_t$$

---

[1] I use this expression, as I have done the corresponding expression in the other case, so as to allow myself the liberty of neglecting qualifications, very properly introduced by Harrod (and by Domar) in their relevant writings, but which for my present purpose have no significance. The relation of my Harrod-type model to Harrod's own will nevertheless be recognized to be closer than that which my Keynes-type model bore to Keynes's.

so that the growth rate of output is s/c. $cg = s$, as (by now) everybody knows.

But before we can use this equation, before we can set it to work, there are several things about it that need to be noticed.

(1) K_t is the value of capital, measured at the fixed prices; we do not need to make any artificial assumption about capital being homogeneous, in order to be able—in this sense—to add capital goods together. But if we interpret K_t in this sense, then $K_t = K_t^*$ is a necessary, but not sufficient, condition of stock equilibrium; for it is possible that the aggregates might be equal, but that the actual stocks of some sorts of capital (in some or all industries) might be greater than desired, these excesses being offset by corresponding deficiencies of other sorts. This is a possibility which one tends to leave out, when one is thinking in 'macro' terms; but here, as we shall find, it is important to be able to refer to it on some occasions.

(2) We do not have to assume that s (the saving coefficient) is constant from period to period; but it is implied in the algebra that c (the capital–output ratio) is the same at the beginning of the period and at the end. In general, however, there is no need for desired capital to depend upon output in any simple manner.

(3) Even if these qualifications are neglected, all that is determined by the Harrod equation is the equilibrium (or 'warranted') rate of growth; but this is not sufficient to determine the equilibrium path. $cg = s$ is simply a flow condition, with the usual properties of flow conditions of equilibrium; in order that it should determine an equilibrium path completely, it needs to be filled out in some way or other. We cannot fill it out as we did in the Keynes-type theory, for there is now no part of the capital stock that is autonomously determined. Some further specification is needed if we are to have a determinate equilibrium path, if only as a standard of reference.

In order to see how this is, let us now suppose that s and c are constant over time. The Harrod equation, treated as a difference equation (just as simple a difference equation as can possibly be conceived), will then have the solution

$$Y_t = (1 + s/c)^t Y_0$$

but this is a path which is not determined until Y_0 is determined. What determines Y_0? As we shall see, this is a question that can be answered in more than one way.

An equilibrium path, let us remember, is a path that will (and can) be followed if expectations are appropriate to it, and if the initial capital stock is appropriate to it; both conditions are necessary. Now it is true that in any *actual* sequence (which may not be an equilibrium sequence) we must begin, at the commencement of period 0 with a capital stock (K_0) that is inherited from the past; in the construction of an actual sequence, from that time onwards this initial stock must be treated as a datum. But in the actual sequence Y_0 is not a datum in the same sense; it may be larger or smaller according as the initial stock is more or less fully employed. If the initial stock is a balanced stock, so that there is some output for which it is the desired stock, that will be the output that is given by the stock condition of equilibrium, $K_0 = cY_0$. One of the ways in which the Harrod equation can be interpreted is to take it as showing the equilibrium path that will be followed if the expectational condition is satisfied, if the initial capital is balanced, and if, in the initial period, it is fully used. The equation to this path might more appropriately be written

$$Y_t = (1 + s/c)^t (K_0/c)$$

a path which (under the above assumptions) is unquestionably fully determined, once K_0 is given.

Such a 'full employment of capital' path is undoubtedly an important concept; we shall be meeting it again in a later chapter.[2] Here, however, I doubt if it is at home. I doubt if this path has any right to be selected as *the* equilibrium path of a Harrod-type model.

For consider what happens if, in the initial period, capital is not balanced, or is not fully employed. (We might alternatively have assumed that the capital stock was employed at more than optimum intensity, for there is no reason to suppose that optimum intensity is the same as maximum capacity.) There will still be an actual production (Y_0) in the initial period. And there will still be an equilibrium path starting from that actual output, the path that would be followed if expectations were right, and if the initial capital had been appropriate, in size and in composition, to this initial output.

But if this path is to be truly an equilibrium path, the initial output must surely be an equilibrium output. We have still not overcome the difficulty.

---

[2] See pp. 136 ff.

A possible way in which the difficulty might be overcome is the following.[3]

K_t, as has been said, is the capital stock at the commencement of period t; Y_t is output during period t. At the commencement of the period, output during the period is *future* output. This we have allowed for; there is stock equilibrium at the beginning of the period (I have repeatedly maintained) if the capital stock at that date is appropriate to this *expected* output. By our condition that in equilibrium expectations are right, we have brought 'expecteds' and 'actuals' together, *along the equilibrium path.* But if it is not an equilibrium path that is being followed, this identity cannot be assumed. It may nevertheless be granted that, even in general, expectations must be founded, in some way and to some extent, upon past experience. If expected output is based upon past output, it is a fair simplification[4] (comparable to that made when we assumed constancy in the original capital–output ratio itself) to reinterpret stock equilibrium to imply that there should be proportionality between the capital stock of time t and the realized output of period $t-1$. We then have

$$K_t = c^* Y_{t-1}$$

as our reinterpreted stock-equilibrium condition. (I mark the new capital–output ratio as c^*, in order to indicate that it is now to be taken in this *ex post* sense.)

It will, however, be noticed that we are making an additional assumption when we take it that expectations are formed in this simple manner. More complex assumptions of the same type (which may well be more realistic) are evidently possible. $K_t = c^* Y_{t-1}$ is merely the simplest form which this relation can take; it is sufficient for most present purposes to take it in this form, but we must not become too dependent on it.

If, however, we accept this relation, and if c^* is to be constant over time (another assumption!), maintenance of stock equilibrium will require that

$$K_{t+1} - K_t = c^*(Y_t - Y_{t-1}) = sY_t$$

[3] I think it is this which Harrod must have had in mind, though it is concealed by his habit of working with continuous time, not divided into periods.

[4] Cf. the assumption about price-expectations that was made in Chapter 7, p. 66 above.

whence it follows that

$$Y_t = \frac{c^*}{c^* - s} Y_{t-1}$$

or
$$c^* g = s(1 + g).$$

Mathematically, this looks hardly different from the Harrod formula; if we shrink the period, so as to work with continuous time, they become identical. But the significance of the revised formula is quite markedly different.

For if, as before, we take our start at time 0 (the beginning of period 0), stock equilibrium requires that $K_0 = c^* Y_{-1}$. And Y_{-1}, since it belongs to the past, is unquestionably given. If the initial K_0 is such as to satisfy this equation, then it is possible that the economy may proceed on an equilibrium path, given by

$$Y_t = (1 + g)^{t+1} Y_{-1}$$

(with g determined by the revised Harrod formula). But if the stock condition $K_0 = c^* Y_{-1}$ is not satisfied, it is not possible for the economy to follow an equilibrium path. If the flow condition is satisfied, the stock condition will never be satisfied. Both conditions must be satisfied if a true equilibrium path is to be followed.

It will be noticed that for this formulation to make sense it is necessary to have $c^* > s$. This looks a harmless condition, which one begins by feeling no difficulty in accepting; for s must be < 1, and one is used to values of the capital–output ratio which are much higher. It must, however, be observed that while s (being a ratio of flow to flow) is a pure number, the capital–output ratio is a ratio of stock to flow; thus the figure that we put upon it depends on the length of the unit period. If we are working with a period of (say) one month, c^* should be very large; but if we change to a 'long' period of (say) five years, the condition $c^* > s$ will be much less obviously satisfied.

It is nevertheless clear that we must have $c^* > s$, whatever the length of the period, if a Harrod-type equilibrium, interpreted as we have interpreted it, is to be possible at all.

This is an important matter; for (as we shall see) the celebrated 'instability' of the Harrod model depends upon it.

Consider an economy that, up to time t (the beginning of period t) has been pursuing an equilibrium path. At that point producers become more optimistic, so that they seek to expand the rate of growth (or, what comes to the same thing, the rate at which they are seeking to accumulate capital). This would be expressed, in the terms which we are now using, by a rise in the *desired* capital–output ratio c^*. The actual capital–output ratio at that time (which is K_t/Y_{t-1}, as we now reckon it) cannot of course be affected, since K_t and Y_{t-1} are already established. It is, however, to be expected that there will be a rise in actual accumulation during period t, above what it would have been if the access of optimism had not occurred. Producers will endeavour to raise K_{t+1}/Y_t towards the desired figure, and the only means that they have at their disposal to do so is to increase investment. But, under the conditions supposed, an increase in investment must have the wrong effect.

Whether or not the economy is in equilibrium, it must always be true that

$$K_{t+1} - K_t = sY_t$$

(for this is an identity). The same relation must hold, for the relevant magnitudes, in the new sequence and in the old (the sequence as it would have been if the access of optimism had not occurred). In order to distinguish, let us say that the access of optimism changes Y_t into $Y_t + \delta Y_t$, and similarly for the other variables. We must then have, in the new sequence

$$K_{t+1} + \delta K_{t+1} - K_t = s(Y_t + \delta Y_t)$$

(for K_t, being the actual capital stock at the moment when the access of optimism occurs, must be unaffected).

Taking the difference of these two equations,

$$\delta K_{t+1} = s\delta Y_t .$$

The realized increase in capital, in the one path over the other, is simply equal to the extra saving. It follows that the realized capital–output ratio, at time $t+1$, must be less, not only than the desired ratio $(c^* + \delta c^*)$, but than the old ratio (c^*). For (along the old sequence) $K_{t+1} = c^*Y_t$ (the old path was an equilibrium path). Therefore

$$\frac{K_{t+1} + \delta K_{t+1}}{Y_t + \delta Y_t} = \frac{c^*Y_t + s\delta Y_t}{Y_t + \delta Y_t}$$

and this must be $< c^*$, since $s < c^*$.

It accordingly follows that in attempting to raise c^*, producers will only have succeeded in lowering it. They will thus, in period $t+1$, have an increased incentive to expand investment, which may be expected to lead to further movement away from the equilibrium path. There is a cumulative divergence from equilibrium.

It is interesting to notice that this 'proof' of instability is not seriously affected if we abandon the assumption that the desired capital depends, in the simple way that we have hitherto taken it to do, upon the output of the previous period only. Suppose, for instance, that it depends upon the average of the outputs of the two preceding periods. We have only to take those two periods together, forming a 'long' period out of them; we can then let the 'long' period stand for the previous period of the model. The whole of the preceding argument will still hold. It must nevertheless be noticed that by lengthening the period we diminish c^*. On the other hand, however much we lengthen the period in this manner, we must still have $c^* > s$; otherwise it would be impossible that an equilibrium path, for a model of this character, should exist at all.

Lagging of this kind does not diminish the instability; it may slow it up (in initial stages), but that is all. It is different if we drop the assumption (on which the whole argument has hitherto depended) that s (the *average* propensity to save) is unaffected by the change in income. That s should be constant along an equilibrium path is perhaps acceptable; but that it should be unaffected when there is a disturbance of equilibrium is rather a different matter. If we rework the equations for the difference between two paths, making s variable, the saving-investment identities will give

$$\delta K_{t+1} = \delta(sY_t)$$

so that the realized capital–output ratio will only fall if

$$c^* > \delta(sY_t)/\delta Y_t$$

which is the *marginal* saving-propensity. It is hardly possible that even this marginal propensity can be greater than unity; thus for a 'short' period (even of quite moderate length) even this stronger condition should be quite readily satisfied. But it is clearly possible that for a 'long' period it might not be; c^* might be less than the marginal, even though it was greater than the average propensity to save. Accordingly, given sufficient lagging *and* a tendency for saving to rise with income (at least when out of equilibrium), the instability of the Harrod-type model could be removed.

A tendency for saving to rise with income (when out of equilibrium) could alternatively be expressed in terms of consumption lags. As is found by other methods, such lags do have a tendency to have a stabilizing effect.[5] But it would certainly appear from the foregoing that, in a Harrod-type model, they would have to be very strong in order to be effective.

There is a remarkable correspondence between the instability of the Harrod-type model, when it is established in this manner, and that of the Wicksell–Lindahl model, when that is established in the manner that was adopted in Chapter 7 of this book. The Wicksellian 'cumulative process' is a property of a Flexprice model, this is a property of a Fixprice model; the one disequilibrium is a price disequilibrium, the other is a quantity disequilibrium; these are exactly the relations that one would expect from 'duals', in something like the sense that Linear Programming theory has made familiar. The more one works it out, the clearer it becomes that there is in fact a duality relation between the two theories.

In the Harrod-type model prices are given exogenously; can one say that in the Wicksell theory quantities are given exogenously? I did not put it that way in Chapter 7 (for it might there have appeared to be too paradoxical a way of putting the point). Something that is substantially equivalent did come up nevertheless. In order that the Wicksell theorem should be true without exception, it was necessary to assume that the 'change in real resources' (as I called it) could be neglected. This amounted to assuming that the sequence of quantities (of inputs and outputs) proceeded autonomously, the sole effect of the discrepancy between actual and 'natural' rates of interest being a movement of prices. That is exactly *dual* to what we have been assuming here.

We further found, in our discussion of the Wicksell theory, that we could not make sense of the sequence without introducing lags, at least to the extent of making price expectations depend upon past experience. So it has been here. We could not make sense of the present story without introducing a similar dependence of expectations upon experience, of demand expectations upon previous output. Here again there is a perfect match.

In the Flexprice model there is cumulative inflation (or deflation) if the expected rate of profit is out of line with actual interest; in the

[5] See, for instance, my *Trade Cycle*, p. 81.

Fixprice model there is cumulative expansion (or contraction) if the expected growth rate is out of line with that which saving makes attainable. The rate of interest in the one theory is dual to the rate of growth in the other.

Among the prices which, in a Fixprice model, are taken to be fixed, is the rate of interest. But the Wicksell model can also be read as a study of the effects of a fixed rate of interest—upon prices, which in its case are flexible. Fixity of the rate of interest (or rather of the whole system of interest and quasi-interest rates) at an arbitrary level is a common feature of both kinds of 'cumulative process'. In the one way or in the other, a system in which interest (in this wide sense) is insufficiently adaptable seems to be liable to go off the rails.

So far, however, this is a mere conjecture. We have much further to go before we can put substance into it.

————————

Let us now return, in the rest of this chapter, to the Fixprice model. We are on the verge of having to abandon it, but there is still one matter which it will be useful to attempt to explore with its aid.

While it is possible for price inflation to proceed to any level,[6] there is ordinarily a limit upon quantity expansion; it must ordinarily be limited by scarcity of primary factors, of which shortage of labour can be taken to be a sufficient example. In practice, of course, such a shortage will have wage- and price-effects, which in a Fixprice theory are excluded from consideration. It is nevertheless useful to see how far we can work out the effects of the shortage entirely 'in real terms' —which is effectively what one does when one examines the problem in a Fixprice model.

Let us then suppose that in a certain period the expansionary path that we have been analysing encounters a full-employment-of-labour 'ceiling'. In order to sharpen the issue, let us take it (here) that the ceiling is an absolute ceiling: the total labour available is absolutely fixed and unchanging over time. We may, I think, take it that once a desired (or optimum) capital–output ratio has been achieved, it will not be possible to increase output without employing more labour.[7] There will thus be an absolute ceiling upon possible output as well as upon labour supply.

—————

[6] There is indeed an interesting correspondence between quantity-expansion arrested by labour shortage and price inflation brought to a stop by limitation of money supply.

[7] The Fixprice assumption must be borne in mind.

Even under these (admittedly drastic) assumptions, there are several cases to be considered.

The first is that, made familiar by Harrod, in which output had been expanding, before the ceiling was reached, along an equilibrium path, more and more of the given supply of labour being absorbed in the course of the expansion. When the absorption is complete, this expansion cannot continue. The desired capital will accordingly cease to expand, and the system cannot remain in equilibrium on its ceiling unless saving halts. If savers attempt to save the same proportion of income as before, output is bound to fall. If the average propensity to save (the proportion of income saved) refuses to decline, output cannot stop falling until it has fallen to zero.

More plausible assumptions about saving behaviour will of course give less apocalyptic results. If the proportion of income saved rises (and falls) with income, there may well be an income (or output) level at which saving is zero; it is then in principle possible for the economy to find a stationary equilibrium at this (no doubt) low level. But it may not be easy to get into that equilibrium. The capital stock which is appropriate to that low level is less than the capital that is appropriate to full employment; thus it is not possible to get into this equilibrium without passing through a phase of decumulation, which will not occur unless output falls to a level which is even lower than its low-level equilibrium. Horrors such as these have been much discussed, and it is probable that they do have some relevance to slump economies. But it is hardly worth while to pursue them far in this place.

For there are other, more interesting, possibilities. One, which arises directly out of the preceding discussion, occurs when the path that has been followed, before the labour ceiling is encountered, is an 'over-optimistic' expansion with an attempted rate of growth which is more than the 'warranted' rate. In this case, as we have seen, actual capital must be less than desired capital, at the point when the labour ceiling is hit. It is then quite possible for the economy to remain in a state of full employment for a certain time, while the deficiency is being made up.[8] The capital–output ratio will then be rising, and output can continue to increase, even though the employment of labour does not increase. For, even at an unchanged output, there would still be an opportunity for the investment of capital to bring the

---

[8] As Kaldor observed, in a justifiable criticism which he made of the corresponding passage in my *Trade Cycle*.

capital–output ratio up to its 'normal' figure; but if investment proceeded in this way, without output rising, the employment of labour would fall. That, however, would leave labour available for an increase in output; the system would have moved down below its full-employment ceiling. There would thus be a further opportunity for productive investment to supply the capital for this increase in output (without further change in the capital–output ratio). As long as the capital–output ratio remains below its 'normal' level, such expansion as this can go on. It is in fact the sort of expansion which was supposed by neo-classical economists to take place while capital increased and the supply of labour remained constant.[9] But it should be emphasized that there is nothing in this argument to indicate that, in the conditions supposed, an expansion of this sort *must* occur; all that has been shown is that it is possible.

And a point must surely be reached (if the deficiency in capital had merely occurred because of over-optimistic investment) when the deficiency is made good. After that (at least so long as we continue to hold by our Fixprice assumptions) all must be as before.

Nevertheless, having got so far, should one not go further? The attribution of the disequilibrium, along the path that was followed (in this last case) before the ceiling was reached to 'over-optimistic expectations', itself depended upon the assumption that at some date in the past the economy had been in an expanding equilibrium, growing at its 'warranted' rate. There is, in general, no need that this should be so. It is by no means necessary to assume that in the macro-economic sense appropriate to a Harrod-type model, a state of stock equilibrium should ever have been attained.

In order to show how this is, something (a very little in this place) must be said about technology. It is only in relation to a given technology (in the sense of a given state of technical knowledge, or available 'spectrum of techniques') that there can be a desired capital corresponding to a particular output—a capital stock which would produce that output in an optimum (or in what is considered to be an optimum) manner. Certainly this is the case if we think of the capital stock in real terms, as consisting of actual capital goods (machines and what not); but even if we think of it in value terms (with the real goods valued at given prices) the truth of the statement is unaffected. It has been implicitly assumed in our analysis (so far) that technology

[9] As Kaldor has also observed.

is unchanging during the process under discussion. I do not in fact see how, in this sort of formal analysis, that assumption is to be avoided. There must nevertheless have been a moment at which this technology was introduced; and it is not interesting to suppose that this moment was in the very remote past. It is much more interesting to take the moment at which the new technology is introduced as the base date from which the process under analysis is to proceed.

The actual capital stock (K_0) at that date will thus have been inherited from the past, from a time at which the technology, under which the economy was working, was different. Whether or not it was appropriate to the old technology, it is inconceivable that it can be appropriate to the new. It cannot possibly be a balanced stock, in relation to the new technology, so that the path which is pursued (from time 0 onwards) cannot possibly be an equilibrium path. Even in value terms, it is entirely possible that K_0 may be greater or less than c^*Y_{-1}, where c^* is the desired (ex post) capital–output ratio of the new technology.

Now suppose (as we are surely entitled to suppose) that, at the moment when the new technology is introduced, full employment of labour had been reached (or almost reached). It does not matter how it was reached—whether along a 'warranted' growth path or in some other way. For all that that will now affect is the relation of actual capital to desired capital under the old technology; and, under the new technology that is irrelevant. All that can now matter is the relation of K_0 to c^*Y_{-1}, the capital which (for the moment) is the desired capital under the new technology.

If, in this sense, $K_0 < c^*Y_{-1}$, we have the same situation as was previously analysed; a neo-classical expansion, up to the point where equality is restored, is clearly possible. But in the opposite case, where it is actual capital that is the greater, there would seem (at first sight) to be no help that way. Would there not then be the same immediate downturn as we deduced for the case in which there was an encounter with a ceiling, after expansion along a 'warranted' (or equilibrium) growth path? If so, we get little comfort from our present way of putting the problem; for it is not obvious that there is any reason (within a Fixprice model) why the crucial inequality should go one way rather than the other.

In fact, however, this is not right. For we have not yet taken into account the necessity (it surely is a necessity) that, in relation to the new technology, the composition of the inherited capital must be wrong. Even if the value of the stock is right, at the old output (if $K_0 = c^* Y_{-1}$), there will still be a potentiality of increased output, as soon as the capital can be replaced in a more suitable form. As that replacement occurs, either output increases or labour becomes unemployed. But if output is to increase, with labour fully employed, capital investment will be required. Thus even if $K_0 = c^* Y_{-1}$, at the moment of introduction of the new technology, there can be some scope for new investment. Some 'neo-classical' expansion is still possible in this case; and the same must presumably hold, though to a lesser extent, if the critical inequality goes, not too far, the 'wrong' way.

And there is (possibly) a further point. We have so far been holding, quite rigidly, to the Fixprice assumption—even so far as to assume that the prices at which capital goods are valued remain the same as they were before, after the new technology has been introduced. But this (surely) is to take 'Fixprice' a bit far. To keep prices fixed while technology is unchanged is (perhaps) tolerable; but it is much more difficult to make sense of the assumption when technology is changing. After all, it was in terms of the pricing of manufactured goods that we introduced the Fixprice assumption originally; but it is on account of changes in technology that the (relative) prices of manufactured goods do most obviously change. Thus we ought surely to go over, when technology changes, to prices that are in some sense more 'suitable' to the new technology. Now, at such prices it seems likely that there will be some existing capital goods (those which had been constructed for specific purposes associated with the old technology) which will be considerably devalued. It looks therefore more likely than it did before that K_0 will be $< c^* Y_{-1}$, when the valuation is made at prices that are 'suitable' to the new technology. Though we still cannot say without exception that active invention is conducive to the maintenance of full employment, it does begin to look as if there is a presumption in that direction.

But what are these 'suitable' prices? This is a question that we cannot answer—cannot even begin to answer—as long as we continue to take prices as given. We have reached the boundary of Fixprice Economics. We must look for a method (whether or not it is the old Flexprice method remains to be seen) which will at least enable us to call prices into question.

13

STRUCTURAL DISEQUILIBRIUM
—TRAVERSE

The chief thing which has emerged from the Harrod-type theory, which was considered in the preceding chapter, is that an economy which has been in long-term equilibrium at fixed prices (which are to maintained) cannot adjust to a change in its desired growth rate, unless the propensity to save is varied, or the capital–output ratio is varied. If (Kaldor's point, of which we took account when we came to it) there is a difference between the propensities to save out of wages and out of profits, and it is these propensities that are fixed, a new equilibrium can be found, provided that there is a suitable change in the rate of profit. Indeed, if *anything* emerges to change the overall propensity to save out of income in the right direction, along any channel, the Harrod difficulty can be got over. And (of course) if the change in the growth rate affects the capital–output ratio in the right direction, that also will help.

But let us now suppose that the Harrod difficulty has been got over: that a suitable change in the propensity to save, for whatever reason, has occurred—will that be the end of the trouble? The magic that used to be attributed to a Keynesian fiscal policy assumed that it would; but there is a school of economists, whose voices were for long almost drowned among the fanfare of the Keynesian orchestra, who have been maintaining, all along, that it is not. They do have something to say; so in this chapter, and in that which follows, I shall look for a method which will give it attention.[1]

In a fixprice macro-theory one looks only at values. Goods that have the same value are treated as if they were the same. So the capital stock is treated as if it were homogeneous; the consumption flow is treated as if it were homogeneous; and the two are treated as if they were homogeneous with one another. (If this were not so, the capital–

---

[1] The story goes back, at least, to Hayek, *Prices and Production* (1932); but there are later statements, such as that of L. M. Lachmann, *Capital and its Structure* (1956), which are closer to what I have in mind.

output ratio would have no meaning.) But of course we know that in fact these things are not homogeneous; each of them is a collection of different things, which at least for some purposes need to be distinguished. From that point of view the fixprice assumption has made things too easy. It has left out the *structure* of the productive system.

The first model which I shall use, to take some account of this structure, is also too simplified, much too simplified; but we shall be able, later on, to find ways of removing at least some of its simplifications. It is only as a first step that we need it. It is just the simplest model which shows up the issues.

Like other macro-economic models, it maintains homogeneity of labour. It maintains homogeneity of *the* capital good, and of *the* consumption good; but these two goods are now different. To remind us that they are to be taken in physical terms, we shall call the consumption good Corn; and the capital good a Tractor. There will thus in the model be two sectors, or industries. On the one hand there will be a consumption good industry, the output of which is Corn, while its inputs are labour and (the use of) Tractors. On the other there will be an investment good industry, the output of which is Tractors, while its inputs are labour and also Tractors.[2]

I shall put the model through its paces, very much as I did with the Harrod-type model. Thus I shall begin with the conditions which have to be satisfied in order that it should continue in an equilibrium—which will here have to be the equilibrium of a steady state, with a constant growth rate. I shall then examine what happens when this equilibrium is disturbed, considering in particular what happens when there is an attempted change in the growth rate. Is it possible, if the structure of the economy, expressed in terms of production coefficients, remains unchanged or if, as we may say, *technique* is unchanged for there to be a smooth passage, or Traverse, to a new equilibrium?

I begin by approaching the question algebraically. Let x be the number of tractor-units, and ξ the number of corn-units, that are pro-

---

[2] To have Tractors appearing as output and also as input in the Tractor-producing industry is uncomfortable; but it is an assumption that is unavoidable, if the model is to contain no more than one capital good. A more general model, with many capital goods, was examined in Chapter XIV of *Capital and Growth*, so far as the steady state of the model is concerned.

It may be remarked, in passing, that the model of that chapter is very similar to the Sraffa model (see note on p. 54 above). But Sraffa's model is a stationary model, in which inputs and outputs are unchanging; mine is a model of a steady state, with constant growth rate.

duced in some particular period.[3] Let a, b, α, β be production-coefficients; a being the tractor-requirement and b the labour-requirement for the production of a tractor-unit; α and β being corresponding coefficients for the production of corn.

Then, for the production of x tractor-units and ξ corn-units

$$K = ax + \alpha\xi, \; L = bx + \beta\xi$$

will be the total requirements of capital and labour respectively. These, the requirement conditions we shall call them, will clearly hold, in terms of requirements, whether the system is in equilibrium or not.

If, however, it is to be in (steady state) equilibrium, there is another condition needed. For the growth rates of x and ξ must then be the same; and so the growth rates of K and L must be the same. The growth rate of L is to be given autonomously; the growth rate of K will have to adjust to it. But what determines the growth rate of K?

There are two points which need consideration, one of capital wastage (we shall not want to suppose that the tractors last for ever) and one of timing. I shall take the latter first.

If there were no capital wastage the capital stock at the end of the period would equal the beginning stock *plus* the new output of tractors (x). It simplifies things if we suppose that new tractors come into use only at the turn from one period to the next;[4] for then we can say that it is the beginning-stock which is to be reckoned to be the input into the production of the period; so it is the beginning-stock which is K. The end-stock, to be used as input into the production of the ensuing period, must then, in equilibrium, be $(1 + g)\,K$. Thus, if there is no capital wastage, we must in equilibrium have $x = gK$.

But if there is capital wastage, replacement of that wastage will have to be made good out of x. So $x = GK$, G exceeding g by an allowance for replacement. We shall permit ourselves to write $G = g(1 + k)$. In a steady state k would have to be constant. In the first stage of our enquiry, we shall keep it as a constant, even out of equilibrium; but that is an assumption which may have to be reconsidered.

---

[3] The practice of using roman letters to refer to the investment goods sector, Greek to refer to the consumption goods sector, was extensively used in *Capital and Growth*. Here we shall not much need it, but it is convenient to follow it.

[4] If the period is no more than a week, tractor are delivered on Saturdays. We can always approach a continuous flow by shortening our period (see below).

We now have three equations, the two requirements equations and an accumulation equation, $x = GK$. From these three x and ξ can be eliminated. For, from the requirement equations,

$$\alpha L - \beta K = (\alpha b - a\beta)x$$

which, from the accumulation equation

$$= (\alpha b - a\beta)\ GK = (\alpha b - a\beta)(1 + k)gK$$

Dividing through by βK, and setting $m = (\alpha b / a\beta)$, $c = (m - 1)(1 + k)$, this gives

$$(\alpha / \beta)(L/K) = 1 + cag$$

the Fundamental Equation of the present model.

When this equation is used as an equilibrium condition, it establishes a relation between the factor-proportion (K/L) and the growth rate, in the steady state. A steady state with that growth rate is possible only if there is this factor proportion which corresponds. But in establishing the equation, g has only been used to mean the growth rate of K, for it is from the accumulation equation that it has been derived. So in that sense the Fundamental Equation will still hold, even out of equilibrium; it can still be used to give the growth of K, though that of L will not be equal to it.

––––––––

We are now in a position to give an answer to the critical question: if the growth rate of L is given autonomously, while an initial factor-proportion is taken arbitrarily, can there be a convergence to equilibrium, along a path where labour and capital are kept fully employed? We shall find that the answer depends upon the sign of c—whether, that is, the corn industry or the tractor industry is the more capital-intensive. If the corn industry is the more capital-intensive, there can be convergence; otherwise not.

I shall begin by providing this proposition algebraically, and afterwards I shall check through the economics.

Consider two consecutive periods, marked t and $t + 1$. In each of these periods the Fundamental Equation must hold. Thus

$$(\alpha / \beta)(L_t / K_t) = 1 + cag_t\ , \quad (\alpha / \beta)(L_{t+1}/K_{t+1}) = 1 + cag_{t+1}$$

But we also have $K_{t+1} = (1 + {}^1g_t)K_t$, and $L_{t+1} = (1 + g^*)L_t$ where g^* is given.

From these four equations we could eliminate the Ls and Ks, getting a difference equation in g_t; but it is neater to eliminate the gs, getting a difference equation in (K/L). So put $(\beta/\alpha)(K/L) = V$.[5] Then $1 + cag_t = (1/V_t)$, so that $ca(1 + g_t) = ca - 1 + (1/V_t)$. Thus

$$\frac{V_{t+1}}{V_t} = \frac{1 + g_t}{1 + g^*} = \frac{ca - 1 + (1/V_t)}{ca(1 + g^*)}$$

and so $V_{t+1} + \lambda V_t + \mu$, where λ and μ depend on ca and g^* alone.

A similar equation must hold along the equilibrium path, where both Vs become V^*. So μ can be eliminated, giving

$$V_{t+1} - V^* = \lambda(V_t - V^*)$$

whence

$$V_t - V^* = \lambda^t(V_0 - V^*)$$

and V_t tends to V^* if λ^t tends to zero as t increases; otherwise not. Now

$$1 - \lambda = 1 - \frac{ca - 1}{ca(1 + g^*)}$$

$$= \frac{1 + cag^*}{ca(1 + g^*)} = \frac{1}{ca(1 + g^*)V^*}$$

All of the elements in this last expression are positive, with the possible exception of c. If c is negative ($m < 1$), $\lambda > 1$ and there is no convergence to equilibrium.

That proves our proposition.[6] But let us look at it again, less mathematically.

---

[5] (K/L) depends upon the units in which K and L are measures; but V is a pure number. For in a period in which no tractors were being produced, $K = \alpha \xi$, $L = \beta \xi$, so that $V = 1$. V is an index of the capital–labour ratios with this *base*.

[6] It proves the important part of our proposition. But it has not yet been shown that if c is positive there must be convergence. This can be shown, subject to an exception, which I think is unimportant, in the following way.

If c is positive, $\lambda < 1$; but could λ be negative? If c were positive and λ negative, ca would be < 1.

Now a, the capital–capital coefficient, is a ratio of stock input to flow output, so it can be indefinitely increased by shortening the length of the period. c, being $(m - 1)(1 + k)$ may indeed be reduced by a reduction in k; but it cannot be reduced beyond $(m - 1)$, which is independent of the length of the period, and (here) necessarily positive. Thus, by shortening (making the input of tractors more continuous, see p. 122 above) ca can be indefinitely increased, so that $ca > 1$ must be satisfied. So in these terms it is not possible for c to be positive and λ negative. For c to be positive is both a necessary and a sufficient condition for convergence.

We start from a steady-state equilibrium, with growth rate g_0, and with supplies of capital and labour which are in a ratio which corresponds. Period 1 begins with supplies (K_1 and L_1) taken over from the old steady state, which are in this ratio; if they are each of them to be fully employed, capital, in period 1, must be accumulated at the old rate g_0. But labour, meanwhile, has had the higher growth rate g^*. So period 2 begins with capital $K_1 (1 + g_0)$ and labour at $L_1(1 + g^*)$—which are not in an equilibrium ratio at either growth rate. If, in period 2, capital continued to be accumulated at the old rate g_0 only that labour which would have been employed in the old steady state can be employed, and that is less than the labour which is available.

If all of the labour is to be employed, even though there is no change in the capital stock—it is still $K_1(1 + g_0)$—there must be a switch in output between the two industries, that of one increasing and of the other diminishing. For it is impossible that the output of both could increase while the supply of capital is given. Capital must be released, from the one or from the other. But a transference of capital, from the one to the other, cannot lead to the desired increase in the demand for labour, unless it is the output of the more labour-intensive, or less capital-intensive, industry, which is expanded by the transference. The output of the other will have to be contracted.

This is why the question of which industry is the more capital-intensive is of such importance. If it is the consumption-good industry which is the more capital-intensive industry ($m > 1$), the transference which is necessary to secure the full employment of labour requires an expansion of the capital-good producing industry. There will thus be accumulation at more than the old rate g_0. Since $g_0 < g^*$, this is a step in the right direction. A similar switch, repeated over several periods, should result in a return, or near-return, to equilibrium.[7] So here there is a full employment path to equilibrium; a successful Traverse can be made.[8]

If, however, it is the capital-producing industry which is the more capital-intensive, the switch, which is necessary to maintain full employment, will require that this is the industry from which capital

[7] In this case $g_1 > g_0$, while $g^* > g_0$; the switch will only lead to a smooth adjustment if $g_1 < g^*$. Otherwise the adjustment overshoots the mark; but there will still be a (damped) oscillation about equilibrium. I have given a reason (in the note on p. 135) why this is a possibility which need not be taken very seriously.

[8] Consumption output is initially reduced, below what it would have been on the old growth, if that had contained. But it grows more rapidly than it would have done on the old growth path, so sooner or later it must overtake.

is withdrawn. That will slow down the rate of expansion of the economy ($g_1 < g_0 < g^*$). This also will have to be repeated in subsequent periods, until the output of the capital-producing industry is reduced to zero. The whole economy will then be in a state of decline, and it will be impossible for an increasing supply of labour to be absorbed. So in this perverse case there can be no Traverse.

A corresponding analysis will apply when the growth rate of labour falls ($g_0 > g^*$); but it does not seem worth while to set it out in detail.

The chief lesson which we learn from these exercises is that smooth adjustment may not be possible.

But that is about all. I am not going to waste time in discussing whether conditions in which m is > 1, or < 1, are the more probable in practice; for it will be my contention that that question does not really arise. Our analysis of the Traverse, in the one-capital-case, is no more than a bogy. It has been useful to work through it, since it should help towards an understanding of what follows. But in itself it is quite misleading. An actual economy—any actual economy—does not, indeed cannot, work just like that. It differs from the model described in quite essential respects. As soon as we take one or two steps nearer reality the situation is greatly transformed.

I do not believe (as I think some economists believe) that the fixity of technique, under which we have been working, is the vital point. The big change occurs before we come to that—at the point where we abandon the single capital good.

I shall confine attention, as before, to the question of a change in the equilibrium growth rate. Such a change will change the equilibrium ratios, not merely between labour and capital in general (whatever that is), but also between one kind of capital good and another. Thus it is not just a question of whether the general (K/L) rises or falls; it is whether a particular (K_i/L) rises or falls; and it will normally be the case that for different capital goods the answer will be different. It would indeed be surprising if (whether g is falling or rising) the equilibrium requirement for labour were to rise more, or fall less, than those for *all* capital goods. Such extreme cases (to which, presumably, the preceding analysis would most closely apply) are so extreme that they are hardly worth consideration. It is safe to assume that some (K_i/L) will rise, and some fall, whichever way the growth rate moves. So that, somewhat surprisingly, a more general theory may turn out to be more straightforward than the 'one capital good' theory.

As in the preceding analysis, we must start with a period 0, in which (if full employment of labour and of all sorts of capital is to be maintained) capital must be accumulated at the same g_0 as in the old equilibrium. But then, at the beginning of period 1, while the capital goods are available in their old proportions, labour will have increased disproportionately (either up or down). Now if, with these quantities of factors, an attempt were to be made (in period 1) to maintain full employment of labour and of *all* capitals, it is most unlikely that the resultant production would be such as to tend towards equilibrium. It is indeed hardly probable that with fixed coefficients, and with all the capital-quantity equations required to hold (essentially as before) but with labour appreciably out of line, a set of positive outputs could be found at all. Something would have to give.

Now if the coefficients are really fixed (more of this in a moment) the existing quantities of capital goods and of labour (still at the beginning of period 1) set constraints on the amounts that can be produced; if we insist on all-round full employment, we are insisting that all of the constraints should be *operative*. If we waive that condition, we can have some constraints operative, but some not. Once there is a choice of the constraints that are to be operative, the set of outputs in period 1 ceases to be determinate; quite a variety of alternatives should normally be open. And some, at least, of these alternatives should be such as to conduct the economy in the direction of an equilibrium.

There is one (sufficiently miserable) alternative which must be open, and which it is useful to take as a standard of reference. If no more than *one* constraint is made operative it is possible for the economy to move on to a constant growth path, at the new equilibrium growth rate, at once. This one operative constraint must be that which is set by the particular capital good for which the ratio of (K_i/L) at the new growth rate and at the old is the lowest. An expansion at the new growth rate, which is 'hinged' upon this particular capital good will certainly be feasible; but under-employment of labour will then be a permanency. This is a feasible path, but it can hardly be called an equilibrium path.

Nevertheless, using this alternative as a basis we can see what is required in order that there should be a better performance. Some of the labour and of the capital goods which, on this 'base' plan are left unemployed, must be directed towards breaking the bottlenecks. There must, that is to say, be a temporary expansion in output, beyond the equilibrium proportion, of those goods that are in shortest supply. Then, as the bottlenecks are relieved, the 'level' of the ultimate equilibrium can be lifted. There may well be some route of this kind, even (I think) with fixed coefficients, by which it can *ultimately* be lifted to a full employment of labour equilibrium level.

Since this 'better' plan involves setting more labour (as well as capital goods) to work than would be set to work under the base plan, it is possible that there might be full employment of labour under the 'better' plan, even throughout. But one cannot be sure of this. There cannot be a 'better' plan unless some resources are under-employed; labour may be among those which are under-employed in the transitional phase, or it may not.

The picture which we have been drawing in this last section is still too dismal; there are several ways in which it needs to be amended, and they all work in the direction of making the Traverse easier. I do not think that these ways ought just to be summed up by saying that we ought to have worked with variable technique. There are variations which ought to be introduced, but they are not all of the same kind, nor do they work in the same way.

The first kind of variation is one that it might have been well to have kept in mind, even in the formal analysis of this chapter. There is no reason why the fixed coefficients should be taken to be representing anything more than the *normal* quantities of inputs required to produce a unit of output. We need not suppose that it would be impossible, at least in the short run, to produce more than 1,000 units of output from the capital stock that is appropriate to 1,000 units. On this 'normal' interpretation it is quite correct to treat coefficients as rigidly fixed so long as we are concerned with equilibrium conditions; but this does not mean that on a Traverse they would have to be rigidly fixed. We have certainly been making them too fixed, so far, in this chapter.

If we bear in mind this interpretation, and rethink the work we have done in the light of it, it becomes evident that there should be a good deal of flexibility, along the Traverse, which has not so far been taken in account. When some capital goods are short, relative to the normal requirement for them, production need not be held down by an insistence that these goods should not be used to more than a normal degree of utilization. They can, at least for a while, be overused. This will raise the total amount of production that can be got from a capital stock that is inappropriately distributed, and in all probability raise it very considerably; for if the scarce goods are used at more than normal capacity, the surplus goods will be less under-utilized than would otherwise be the case.

That, however, leads on to the second point. If the scarce goods are over-utilized it is to be expected that they will be used up faster. In the case of circulating capital goods, over-utilization means reducing stocks below normal. There is a limit beyond which that process can-not be carried, and (even short of that limit) the deficiency must, sooner or later, be made up. In the case of fixed capital, there will also be some tendency to more rapid wear and tear; the future need for replacement will, at least to some extent, be increased. There is much the same effect on either side.

Nevertheless, even if one grants that over-utilization means 'bor-rowing from the future', it does facilitate greater flexibility. Indeed, the whole process of using-up and replacement is a source of flexibility, since when additional supplies of some good are (for a time) no longer required, it is not merely net investment in that good, but gross in-vestment, that can be cut down to zero. Too much, however, should not be made of this, since it cuts both ways. While it increases the resources that are made available for transference, it also increases the resources which must be transferred, if idleness of capital is to be kept as low as possible. It may well be that a more important source of flexibility arises in connection with those goods which are *in the middle*, being neither made particularly scarce nor particularly surplus by the change that has occurred. Normal replacement of such goods (and a normal expansion in their supply) will indeed be required, if not now, then later; but if it is possible to postpone it, so that the resources which would be used for it can be (temporarily) employed elsewhere, bottlenecks which would otherwise have been cramping may be more speedily broken.

All this (as I think the reader will agree) does sound like sense—much more like sense than was the case with the 'simple' model with which we began this chapter. But (I expect he will be burning to ask) what about prices? Surely we must say something about prices if we are to tell anything like a full story.

I have deliberately posed the problem of this chapter in terms of a change in the (equilibrium) growth rate; for, in terms of equilibrium analysis, a change in g has the special quality that (if it is matched by a suitable change in the saving-propensity) prices do not *need* to be affected by it. In this case (and only, I think, in this case) prices in the new equilibrium can be the same as they were in the old. But does this mean that prices can remain unchanged on the way—along the Traverse?

It is by no means inconceivable that most prices might remain unchanged along the Traverse. For that, I think, is precisely the behaviour which is implied by 'full cost pricing' (or, as I would myself prefer to call it, *normal cost pricing*) in the present application. On this policy the prices which producers set are what they think to be equilibrium prices; they stick to those prices even when they are out of equilibrium.

With such behaviour, the account of adjustment which we gave when we were dealing with the Fixprice method[9] does (at least roughly) hold; the adjustment is being made in what is substantially a Fixprice manner, with prices playing no active part. And it is important to emphasize that adjustment can be made (some, at least, of the required adjustment can be made) even if it is only made in this particular way. For in the first place (since we are *not* assuming textbook perfect competition, such that marginal cost rises, immediately the equilibrium output is passed) there will be some output, beyond the equilibrium output, which producers will be only too glad to produce, once there is a demand for it. Secondly, even though they behave in a thoroughgoing Fixprice manner, setting (for accounting purposes) normal prices on their inputs as well as on their outputs, it will be a fact that capacity that is under-utilized will not be earning a full profit: if production can be stepped up profit will be increased. There is an incentive to bring unutilized capacity into production, and to extend production (when there is a demand) some way beyond optimum output, even when there is no movement in prices.

Yet if the adjustment proceeds entirely on this plan, there are limits to what can be done. Though there is an incentive, even in a Fixprice system, to bring into production unused capacity (not only fixed capital capacity, but surplus stocks of materials) when it can be utilized by its present proprietor; and though resources that are wholly unused may be transferred, since it is better to get the fixed price for them than to leave them idle; the mechanism of transference from those whose need is less to those whose need is more urgent must unquestionably be clogged. I am not thinking here of consumers' needs (all

[9] Above, pp. 128–9.

that is being taken for granted—formally, we still have our one consumption good!); the urgency in question is urgency in the breaking of bottlenecks. Flexibility along the Traverse is of major importance; an economy which insists upon making its transitions on a Fixprice basis is doing so with 'one hand tied behind its back'.

It is this that is the true function of price-flexibility along the Traverse: not, as economists have sometimes supposed, that it can itself give much guidance about the planning of production, about the choice of a path to equilibrium. This is another of the points that I have tried to bring out by my choice of a change in g as the key variable to be studied; for that is a case which is such that, even if there is a change in prices during the transition, the old price will have to be restored when equilibrium is restored.[10] If there is no change in prices during the transition, the choice of which path to pursue (out of the many paths that will be available, once we recognize that some capital goods will have to be surplus) depends entirely on the foresight of producers, on their skill in interpreting what has been happening to them, on their ability to forecast demand. If prices vary during the transition the position is not much better. For the changes in prices that will occur, during a transition of the kind that we are examining, are essentially temporary; operation with prices that are varying, and are (or ought to be) known to be varying, is a task that requires the same kind of skill as the corresponding operation on the quantity side.

When we are considering a different kind of Traverse, which is such that the price ratios that are appropriate to the new equilibrium and to the old are not the same, a corresponding *Fixprice* policy would presumably imply that prices are adapted at once (or sought to be adapted at once) to the new equilibrium; this is an adjustment that could be made (if people were clever enough), unlike the corresponding adjustment on the quantity side which (in this case) probably could not be made at all.[11] But even if the 'right' prices could be reached immediately, and were then held, the position would be the same as with the Fixprice policy after the change in growth rate. The arguments about flexibility on the way to equilibrium remain substantially the same.

[10] I assume (as elsewhere in this chapter) that saving is adjusted to the new growth rate.

[11] In the case of a change in the growth rate, it would be possible to move at once along the constant growth rate path which we took as 'base', though that would not be an equilibrium path. If the change was one (say) in technology, even that 'miserable' alternative would not be possible.

But there is a far larger question that then comes up. It is a condition for the establishment of the new equilibrium that the right prices
should be found—for without the establishment of the right prices the
right techniques will not be selected. If it is not just a matter of the
maintenance of the old prices, but of the finding of new prices, this (in
turn) cannot be an easy matter. If unsuitable prices are adopted, and
adhered to for long, unsuitable techniques will be adopted; the problem of getting into equilibrium will be further complicated, and the
approach to equilibrium will be retarded.[12]

In an actual economic situation, all these problems arise at once,
while (because of the advance in technology) the equilibrium at which
the economy is aiming is continually shifting. No wonder that there is
a problem of business management!

[12] I am thinking of the choice of techniques as being properly a matter of the long-
term equilibrium; short-period adjustments being not so readily expressible in terms
of production coefficients. But there can, of course, be no firm line. Cases may arise
(they are not so infrequent in conditions of changing technology) in which an arrange-
ment, which would quite conveniently be expressible in terms of production coefficients, may be temporarily adopted to fill the gap until a superior technique has been
more fully worked out, or until the new capital goods (which take long to produce) are
ready.

14

TRAVERSE AGAIN:
THE AUSTRIAN METHOD

The last of the methods which I shall be examining is a counterpart to its predecessor. It also is concerned with structure, with structural rigidities, and with Traverse; but the rigidities which it emphasizes are different.

When the former method was being looked at by itself, we did not need a name for it; but now that we are to have another which is to be contrasted with it, both must be named. Each, it so happens, can be named from its ancestry. There already existed, at the end of the nineteenth century, two alternative ways of modelling a whole economy: the general equilibrium of Walras, and the intertemporal method of the Austrian school, whose leader on this matter was Böhm-Bawerk. The requirement equations, on which our former method was based, used the coefficients of production of Walras: they were questions of a type that was used by Walras, so we may label the former method Walrasian. That which I shall be describing, very briefly, in this chapter, is similarly descended from the Austrian.

The Walrasian equations, as Walras used them, were quite static; but we tried to give them a time reference by insisting that they referred to a period of time, with beginning and end. Inputs went in at the beginning, outputs came out at the end. A sequence of periods could then, it appeared, be strung together by matching the end of one period with the beginning of its successor. But just what was supposed to happen at the join?

We had to suppose, when analysing a Traverse, that capital (tractors) could be transferred, in various quantities, from one 'industry' to another, between one period and the next. If the end of the one and the beginning of the other are simultaneous, the transfer must take place instantaneously. But that is quite hard to accept. (Marshall, assuredly, would not have let us have it.)

One gets no help, it should be noticed in passing, from the celebrated device of von Neumann, according to which the whole of the terminal capital (of the period) is treated as output of the period, while the

initial capital is treated as input. For it remains the case that it must
be possible, at the join, for the capital to be reallocated. Von
Neumann's device is quite acceptable, and very useful, so long as we
confine attention to equilibrium paths—in the sense of paths where
the whole course of production, over many periods, is being planned
at the start and is being carried through. Instantaneous reallocation
may well be practicable if it is planned reallocation. But this will not
do for Traverse analysis, for the study of what happens when an equilibrium is disturbed.

The basic element of a (modern) Austrian theory is a process of production, extending over time. There is a stream of inputs, extending
over time, which is transformed into a stream of outputs, also extending over time. Since it is the intertemporal relations in which we are
interested, the inputs are taken to be otherwise homogeneous; they
are just a flow of 'labour'. The outputs also are taken to be homogeneous—just as the consumption good was taken to be homogeneous
in our form of the Walrasian model.

So it is only the inputs of labour and the outputs of final product to
which we pay attention. Some of the labour, indeed, will be turning
out intermediate products, on which more work will be done at a later
stage of the process; some of these intermediate products will be durable instruments, others will be used up when they are used. But all
that is *inside* the process. It is just the stream of labour inputs and the
stream of final product outputs which define the process.

The process must be taken to have a beginning; for if not, how
could a new process ever be adopted? It is not so evident that it must
have an end. It is nevertheless the case that on a Traverse, from an
equilibrium where the economy is adjusted to one technique to one
where it is adjusted to another (if such exists), old processes must be
discontinued. So it makes for simplicity in statement to treat all processes as being 'mortal'. There is thus an analogy between a 'population' of processes and a human population. Some of the concepts
which apply to the one will apply to the other.

What corresponds to the coefficients of production of a Walrasian
model must here be the *profile* of a unit process

$$(a_0, a_1, \ldots a_n; b_0, b_1, \ldots b_n)$$

as written out. The as are labour inputs, the bs are outputs of final
product, each of them dated by their suffixes. Such a profile will

define a *technique*. The scale of production, using that technique, can be changed by multiplying each constituent by a common factor (x).[1]

In a steady state, the technique of production remains the same over time; so all the processes that are alive must have the same profile. But they must have been started at different dates, for only so can the composition of the population of processes remain unchanged over time. It will be sufficient if the starts have been increasing at a constant rate (g), which will then emerge as the constant growth rate of the whole economy.

For then x_T, the number of starts in period T, will be $x_0(1 + g)^T$, or $x_0 G^T$, if we write G for $(1 + g)$, as will be convenient. The employment of labour in period T, A_T, will then be made up from $a_0 x_T$ from processes started in the current period, *plus* $a_1 x_{T-1}$ from processes started one period back, and so on, back to $T - n$. (We do not need to go further, since processes started further back are dead.) Thus

$$A_T = a_0 x_T + a_1 x_{T-1} + \; \ldots \; a_n x_{T-n}$$
$$= x_T(a_0 + a_1 G^{-1} + a_2 G^{-2} + \; \ldots \; a_n G^{-n})$$

in the steady state. The bracketed expression is independent of T, so A_T is proportional to x_T, and has the same growth rate.

In the same way, with B_T output in period T,

$$B_T = x_T (b_0 + b_1 G^{-1} + \; \ldots \; b_n G^{-n})$$

so the ratio (B_T/A_T) is constant over time. It is a basic characteristic of production by the technique which is in question. It seems appropriate to call it the *current productivity* of the technique, for it is productivity, in terms of current output, of the current labour which is being applied.

Current productivity, in a steady state, depends on the technique, and on the growth rate at which it is being operated. With given technique, it is a function of g. This relation could be drawn out as a curve, which I call the *efficiency* curve of the technique. It shows the way in which current productivity will vary, from one steady state to another, when the same technique is used in each, but the growth rate of the starts is different.

---

[1] This is an assumption of constant returns to scale, which cannot here be avoided. I fully accept that it is a weakness, but I think that this is compensated for some purposes (and that is all that is being claimed) by other advantages.

It is natural to suppose that it would be a downward-sloping curve. For the higher the growth rate, the larger will be the proportion of current resources that are being devoted to future output, and the less to current output. But this is hardly a proof of the downward slope; we can do better by proceeding indirectly.

In order to do this, we must fill out the model by introducing prices. There is room in the model for two markets: a Labour Market, on which labour is exchanged for current product (for there is nothing else in which the labour can be paid), and an intertemporal market, most conveniently understood as a market on which product, to be supplied at one date, is exchanged for product to be supplied at another. So there are two prices—a rate of wages (w) and a rate of interest (r).

In these terms we can find the condition for a process to be profitable (or viable). This is that the process should transform current product into future product (by paying current product to labour, and using the labour to produce future product) at least as effectively as the transformation could be directly performed on the market.

In period t from the start of a process, input is a_t and output b_t; so the surplus (or deficit) in that period is $b_t - wa_t$, where w is the rate of wages. I shall write this q_t. The test for a process being viable, at wage w and rate of interest r, is that the stream of qs, discounted (or accumulated) at this rate of interest, to any date, should be non-negative. It is convenient to take the discounting back to the start of the process, so the test is that

$$k_0 = q_0 + q_1 R^{-1} + q_2 R^{-2} + \ldots q_n R^{-n}$$

where R is written for $(1 + r)$, should be non-negative.

Since as and bs are constant, for a given technique, k_0 is a function of w and r. Every q_t is diminished by a rise in w, so k_0 must be diminished by a rise in w if r is unchanged. It is not so obvious that k_0 must be raised by a fall in r (since we shall clearly not want to assume that all qs are positive). It can however be shown[2] that if we do not make

---

[2] Let k_t be the value of the tail of the process, discounted back to its beginning at time t. The truncation assumption can be taken to imply that all k_t are positive, from $t = 1$ to n. We have

$$k_t = q_t + q_{t+1} R^{-1} + \ldots q_n R^{-(n-t)}$$

so that $k_t = q_t + K_{t+1} R^{-1}$. It follows that k_t is bound to rise, for a fall in r, if k_{t+1} is positive and is not reduced by the fall in r. A similar argument holds for k_{t+1}, and so on, up to k_n. But k_n (by truncation) is necessarily positive; it equals q_n, so it is unaffected by the fall in r. So k_{n-1} must be raised, and so on, back to k_0. (See *Capital and Time*, pp. 17–21, for a fuller discussion.)

the duration (n) of the process invariable, but let it be cut short (truncated) if the remainder (or 'tail') of the process ceases to be profitable, it will always be true that k_0 will be increased by a fall in r, and diminished by a rise in r. I shall make this assumption.

It must always be the case that a sufficient rise in r will cause k_0 to become negative.[3] Thus a process which is viable at some r and some w will always have its k_0 reduced to zero if revalued at some higher rate of interest. We may regard this rate as that which is proper to the technique (at given w); it is the 'internal rate of return'.

In a steady state, where there is full adjustment to the technique that is used, and w remains constant, the market rate of interest must be equal to this proper rate. For if the market rate were higher, no new processes of this kind could get started; while if it were lower, a capital gain could be got for nothing on the mere announcement of the intention to start a process. Thus, the market rate of interest is determined by the condition that r and w are such that $k_0 = 0$.

Now, if we write this condition in full, putting $b_t - w a_t$ for each q_t and rearranging, it appears as

$$(b_0 + b_1 R^{-1} + \ldots b_n R^{-n}) = w(a_0 + a_1 R^{-1} + \ldots a_n R^{-n})$$

This shows w as a function of r; and it is *exactly the same* function of r as current productivity (B/A) was of g. So it is just the same *efficiency curve* which shows both relations. We have shown that (given Truncation) the curve must be downward-sloping on the (w, r) interpretation; so it must be downward-sloping on the other interpretation also.

That makes sense. For consider Fig. 2, where the curve is drawn out on a diagram. r and g are measured on the vertical axis, w and (B/A) on the horizontal. If g is less than r (as drawn), it follows from the downward slope that (B/A) is greater than w. So B is greater than wA; current output is greater than what is paid out in wages. There is a surplus which is not paid out in wages, but otherwise consumed. If there had been no such 'take-out', so that the whole of the current product had been reinvested, the growth rate would have been equal to the internal rate of return, as happens in many other growth models (from Adam Smith[4] onwards).

It is bound to be tempting, having got so far, to use the efficiency curve in a conventional (static) manner. By comparison between the

---

[3] We shall want to take it that b_0 is zero, so that q_0 is negative. By a sufficient rise in r, R^{-1} will tend to zero, so that k_0 must go negative.

[4] p. 311.

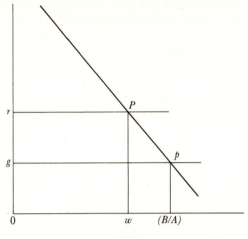

Fig. 2

curves which belong to a pair of techniques, we can show the changes involved in a movement, from a steady state at the one technique to a steady state at the other. 'Other things', saving propensities and the growth rate of the labour supply, are independent and can be kept unchanged. The former may be taken to mean that, with $g = sr$ (as in other growth models), s is unchanged. From the latter, g is unchanged. The 'ultimate' effects of a change in technique, then, can be read off from the diagram, by considering the points at which rP and gp (the horizontals through r and g) meet the new efficiency curve.

There is much to be said on this use of the apparatus, but I shall not pursue it here, since it is not in the spirit of the Austrian method. How do we know that, after a new technique is introduced, there will be convergence to a new equilibrium? And what will happen on the way? These, unlike the other, are traverse questions, for the consideration of which the Austrian method is suitable. I shall explain a little of what can be done about them.

Consider an economy, of the kind that has been described, which has been fully adjusted to an *old* technique. It is convenient to suppose it to have been in a steady state at that technique, though that may not be strictly necessary. What is essential for the full adjustment is that all of its processes, which are *alive* at the beginning of period 0, use that old technique. Then, at that point, a new technique becomes available, or is *invented*. It is more profitable than the old technique at the current rate of wages; so, for starts in period 0, it is adopted. If the rate of wages does not change, and there is no further invention, it will go on being used for starts, as far ahead as we care to look. Even so, there will be a time (which it will be fair to think of as quite a long time) when processes, using the old technique, still remain alive. I call this phase, during which both old and new techniques are in use, the Early Phase of the Traverse. (For we must not take it for granted that when the Early Phase is completed, there will be an easy convergence to a new steady state.)

Most of the rest of what I have to say, in this place, will refer to the Early Phase. It is surely proper to give that our main attention, since the coexistence of 'modern' and 'obsolescent' processes is so normal a phenomenon in the world in which we live.

There are three questions which, in Early Phase theory, we seem called on to examine:

(1) How will things work out if the wage (a real wage, it will be remembered) remains fixed, just where it was in the old equilibrium? The new technique has become the more profitable at that initial wage, so for new starts it is adopted. There is no further invention, so it goes on being adopted. I call this the Fixwage path. Along this path employment is a variable.

(2) How will things work out if employment is constrained to move just as it would have moved if the old steady state had continued? Here it is the wage that will have to be variable. Nevertheless, one supposes that the same technique, which at time 0 became dominant, continues to be dominant in spite of the changes in wages that are likely to occur. I call this the Full Employment path.

(3) How will things work out if the change in wages provokes a further change in technique, or further changes, changes which are *induced* by the change in wages? This is surely the most interesting of these questions; on it, we shall find, there are important things to be said. We consider the others, mainly, as preliminaries to it.

It will be found, in all of these cases, that in period 0 the rate of interest will rise. For, as we have seen, the rate of interest must equal the rate of return on the new processes being started; and it is a condition for the adoption of the new technique that the rate of return on it should be higher. (It may well happen that as a result of the rise in interest some old processes are truncated. This may happen, but it does not have to happen; I shall leave it out.)

We then find that the 'tails' of the old processes are continuing, just as they would have done if the invention had not occurred. So we are at liberty to use the path which *would have* been followed if the invention had not occurred, as a *reference path* with which the new path can be compared. We can concentrate attention on the differences, in employment and output, between the new path and the reference path. And these (if the possibility of truncation is overlooked) are solely a matter of the differences between the processes that are started, at time 0 and subsequently, on the one path and on the other.

I shall use stars to mark magnitudes which refer to the reference path, those referring to the new path being left unstarred. Thus interest rises from r^* to r; A_T *is employment at time T* on the new path, A^*_T is employment on the reference path, and so on.

I shall further take it that in both processes considered, $b_0 = 0$; no process produces final output in the period when it is started. (So we are only concerned with what the older Austrians reckoned as 'capital-using production'; no process yields output at once.) It follows that in period 0 all output comes from old processes: $B_0 = B^*_0$.

We now have the material with which to sketch out answers to our three questions.

(1) *The Fixwage path.* The rate of starts is here unconstricted by shortage of labour; it is nevertheless constricted by shortage of funds with which to pay labour, funds which must take the form of newly produced final product, available for reinvestment, being not otherwise consumed. Thus, in order to determine the rate of starts, on which employment and output depend, we have to make some assumption about saving. The easiest assumption to take as standard is what I shall call the Take-out hypothesis (TH). This is that 'Take-out', the part of the current produce which is not reinvested, remains the same on the actual as it would have been on the reference path. This is surely, in the Early Phase, a defensible assumption. It follows from it that in every period

$$B_T - w\,A_T = B_T^* - w\,A_T^*$$

In period 0, as shown, $B_0 = B_0^*$; so, with constant w, $A_0 = A_0^*$. With no truncation of the older processes, this gives $a_0 x_0 = a_0^* x_0^*$. All that can happen, in period 0, is that the labour which would have started old-type processes, on the reference path, is transferred on the actual to start new-type processes.

We can thus choose units, for the present discussion, such that the labour which is transferred in period 0 is one unit of labour. And we can also choose units so that each of the processes that is started is a unit process. So a_0, a_0^*, x_0, x_0^* can all of them be set equal to unity.

The profile of each process, written out again, with the simplifications which are now at our disposal, will be of the form

$$(1, a_1, a_2, \ldots a_n; 0, b_1 \, b_2, \ldots b_n)$$

What happens in subsequent periods depends on the relation between the two sequences of these remaining as and bs.

It could be that all the as were the same on the one technique and on the other. Then, since the new is to be the more profitable, at current w, some at least of the bs must be larger than their corresponding b^*. Suppose that $b_1 > b_1^*$. Then $B_1 > B_1^*$; for $B_1 - B_1^* = b_1 x_0 - b_1^* x_0^*$ (the b_0s are zero) and both of the xs are unity. $B_1 - w A_1$ is to be unchanged (by TH hypothesis); so $A_1 > A_1^*$. There is already, in period 1, an *increment* in employment.

It could be, on the other hand, that the bs are unchanged between the two techniques but that some of the as are diminished. Suppose that a_1 is diminished. Since b_1 is unchanged, there will be no change in B_1, and therefore (from TH) no change in A_1. But $A_1 = a_0 x_1 + a_1 x_0 = x_1 + a_1$ (on our convention); so if a_1 is diminished, x_1 must be raised. Less labour is absorbed in furthering the processes that were begun in period 0; so the funds which are needed for paying that labour are diminished and funds are available for starting new processes. There is an increment of starts in period 1; this will lead to increments in output, and in employment, in later periods.

Any further increments in bs, or decrements in as, will set up similar effects, which will go on. So if the improvement just takes the form of increasing some bs, or of diminishing some as, or both, the growth of the economy must be raised (perhaps after a lag) above what it would have been on the reference path—above, that is, what it was in the old steady state.

There is however no necessity that things should work out so smoothly. There must in the end be an increment in surpluses, if the change in technique is to be profitable; but it need not persist all the time, all along the series. It could happen, in particular, that the additional output, or the cost-saving, which would ultimately come from the change, might be much deferred. Suppose, for instance, that output, which appeared in period 1 from the start of an *old* process, did not appear in the *new* until period 2. Then B_1 is zero, while $B_1{}^*$ is positive; so (by TH) $A_1 < A_1{}^*$. There must then be fewer starts in period 1 than there would have been on the reference path; this check also will be carried forward. Nevertheless, the switch to the new process being profitable, there must be positive surpluses emerging sooner or later which will come to the rescue.

Much the same will happen if the new process absorbs a lot of labour, relatively to the other, in its opening stages; for this also will show, in our notation, in the form of early bs being less than their corresponding b^*s. So here also there will be a check to the growth of output, and of employment, near the beginning of the Early Phase—to be matched by greater expansion later on.

That such a check is a possibility was first noticed by Ricardo, in the celebrated chapter 'On Machinery', which he added to his *Principles* when he came to revise it. One can easily see that a change in technique, which takes the form of an increase in mechanization, is very likely to fit into the pattern which has just been described. The use of more fixed capital, in order to economize on circulating capital, implies using more labour near the start of the process in order to use less later. This will lead to a (temporary) contraction in final output; and that must be matched by a (temporary) decline in employment, unless there is some source from which the additional savings, which are needed to maintain employment at constant (real) wages, can be found. We know by experience that developing countries need, very usually, to borrow abroad to support the first stages of a development process: that fits in.

(2) *The Full Employment path.* The rates of start are here constricted, directly, by labour supply; so, in formal terms, they are determined directly by the input-coefficients (a_t), the output-coefficients (b_t) having nothing to do with them. Thus from $A_0 = A_0{}^*$, we have $a_0 x_0 = a_0{}^* x_0{}^*$; or, on our former convention on units, $x_0 = 1$, as before. From $A_1 = A_1{}^*$, with the same notation, $x_1 + a_1 = x_1{}^* + a_1{}^*$. So x_1 is determined; and later xs will be determined in the same way.

When xs are determined, with given bs, outputs (B_T) will be determined. Since $Q_T = B_T - w A_T$, what is available for Take-out will thus depend on w. If, as we have been supposing, the Take-out is fixed, it is the wage which will have to adjust, for there is nothing else.

So what corresponds to the check to employment on the Fixwage path (when the improvement is of a Ricardo-machinery type) must here be a *sag* in wages. Later on, when the improvement leads to a rise in current productivity, as it must if it is to be profitable, wages will rise; but for the time being there is a sag.

It will be noticed that on the Full Employment path, as here defined, wages are directly affected by saving propensities, just as on the Classical Wage Fund doctrine they were supposed to be. It was not a step forward when that doctrine was entirely discarded by post-classical economists. It is a valid doctrine, in its place. It is true that current output is largely predetermined by decisions that have been made in the past. So if there is no source from which (real) wages can be paid, except from current output, what is available for wages depends on Take-out, on the share of current output that is taken off for other purposes. Of course it is true that in practice there are other sources—drawing on stocks or borrowing from abroad—which may be called on for relief, for a time. Much attention to these has been paid on our former *methods*; but we also need a method such as the 'Austrian' which does not rely upon them.

(3) *Induced invention*. Let us now go on to the stage—which must be reached sooner or later on a Full Employment path with restricted supply of labour (even if there is a Ricardo-machinery effect)—when the wage rises. Then, if the same technique continues to be adopted for new processes, the rate of profit (or interest) must fall. It must fall in the way that is shown by the efficiency curve of the technique in question. It may then happen that another technique, which it would not, at a lower rate of wages, have been profitable to adopt, becomes profitable. This shift in technique, which comes about as a result of the change in wages that *has occurred*, may properly be described as an *induced invention*.[5]

Consider how this appears on our efficiency-curve diagram, here redrawn as Fig. 3. The *w* and the *r* that were established, when the economy was adjusted to its *old* technique, are represented by the

---

[5] When the term induced invention is interpreted statically (as was done, for instance, in my own *Theory of Wages* of 1932) it raises horrid problems about distinction between techniques, which are known but not used because they do not pay at current prices, and techniques which are not known but are discovered when prices change. In the former case they are said to be 'within the technology', in the latter not. But 'unchanged technology' is a static concept; in dynamic analysis we do not need it. It is surely the case that in practice every shift in technique, if it is of any importance, requires new knowledge, or new expertise. So every shift, which comes about as a consequence of a change in wages (or, more generally, in scarcities) may be properly reckoned to be an induced invention.

It will be noticed that on this interpretation, there can be no 'reswitching'; every switch in technique is a switch to something new (*Capital and Time*, pp. 39–46, 120–1).

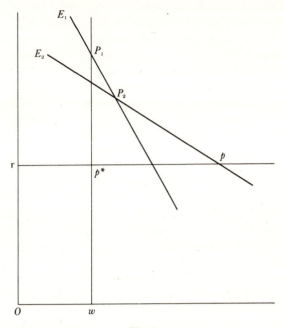

Fig. 3

point P^*. (We do not need to draw the old efficiency curve.) E_1 is the efficiency curve of the first new technique. Initially, as we have seen, the adoption of the new technique for new processes started does not change the wage; so there is just a rise in r, from P^* to P_1. Later, however (perhaps, from what has been said, not at all immediately) the expansion which is promoted by the higher profit will raise the wage; so the 'representation' moves downward along the curve, towards P_2. We are now to suppose that after P_2 is reached, another technique becomes more profitable. The relation between the efficiency curves, E_1 and E_2 must then be as shown.

It must be as shown, since the switch is not profitable at a lower wage (to the left to P_2) but is more profitable at a higher wage (to the right). This must be so, but the consequences of it being so are at first sight peculiar.

The switch occurs because labour has become so expensive; so it must be directed towards saving labour. It reduces the pressure on the labour market, so it must restrain the rise in wages. Yet it looks from the diagram as if a movement to the right along E_2 yields a higher wage than a movement along E_1. But one should not jump to that conclusion, for nothing is said by the diagram about the rate at which the representation moves on the one curve and on the other. It is perfectly possible that *at a particular time* the wage is lower on E_2, after the switch, than it would have been at the same time on E_1. It is perfectly possible that the movement along E_2 may be slower.

There are indeed good reasons for thinking that this, for a while, may be the case. For the switch from E_1 to E_2, when the curves are related in the way that is shown, is very likely to have the same bias as that which produces the Ricardo-machinery effect.[6] It may not be enough to cause an actual fall in wages at the switch-point, but it may yet be enough to check the rise.

Even so, the higher profits, which are gained by switching to E_2 instead of continuing on E_1, facilitate more expansion; and the expansion that is possible along E_2 is greater than what is possible along E_1. When the expansion has proceeded so far as to bring r to the same level on the one path as on the other (in an ultimate steady state, if that is attainable), w on E_2 must be higher. That is what the diagram says, and it is not incorrect.

Though the initial effect of an induced invention, induced by the need to combat a shortage of labour, may be expected to be unfavourable to labour, its longer-run effects are likely to go the other way. More is obtainable by expansion, along a path which has greater expansionary potential, than can be obtained by refusal to make the initial sacrifice that is needed to transfer to it. Since no characteristic of actual labour has been used in this discussion, save that it is an input into the productive process (and not an output) this is a principle of a very wide general application.

———————

So where we have come to, on this Austrian route, is close to Ricardo. Not to the static method which he so largely bequeathed to his successors, but to his latest insights, which he did not live to follow up. The Austrian method is indeed a Classical method; it is classical because it so naturally applies itself to those big problems with which the Classics were mainly concerned: how does economic growth come about? how, when started, can it be maintained?

[6] This is proved, for a special case (but in all probability an important case) in *Capital and Time*, p. 113. An attempt to move in the direction of a more general demonstration is made in the same book, p. 141.

It would have been clearer that these were Ricardo's problems if he had not started his story in the middle. Shortage of land, he shows, makes the profit rate decline; but how is it able to decline? How has it been, initially, so high that decline from that height is possible? Ricardo's story makes better sense if one starts further back—from the making of an invention, which may be scientific, or from some other kind of increase in knowledge. The initial effect of this is to offer opportunity for exceptional profits, which give an impulse to expansion. From any one such impulse, Ricardo is showing, no more than limited expansion is likely to be possible; for the expansion will encounter scarcities by which it will be checked. Shortage of land, of which Ricardo made so much, is no more than one of the possible scarcities. The check may also come from shortage of labour—or indeed from shortage of particular kinds of labour—or of natural resources.

But that, in a favourable case, may be no more than a beginning; for impulses breed—one begets others. Some of these secondary impulses are technological consequences: in the application of the primary impulse, new opportunities are found. But there are also some which are bred by the scarcities. These are the 'induced inventions', on which we have found that the Austrian method has much to say.

Its ability to face up to such classical problems gives the Austrian method its strength. It nevertheless shares, with the Classics, with Ricardo and also with Smith, what appears from a Keynesian standpoint to be a major weakness. Though it can take account of structural unemployment, it cannot allow for Keynesian unemployment—for the under-functioning which Keynesian economics is about. It has, very obviously, nothing to say about money; but that is not all. Even a barter economy, if such is conceivable, could under-function, for there can be piling up of unsold stocks of goods, as well as of idle balances. To all such things as these it turns a blind eye.

I have made no claim throughout this book, that any of the methods I have been considering will do for all purposes. I have given much attention to Keynesian methods, in Chapters 6–12 above, since I do believe that there are most important problems for the study of which they do have a place. There are others, however, for which they are not so appropriate. We have learned by sad experience, especially since 1970, that there are structural rigidities that do not yield at all easily to Keynesian remedies, or indeed to any sort of monetary remedy. If we are to think clearly about them we need other methods. I claim no more for the Austrian method, considered in this chapter, and for the Walrasian, considered in its predecessor, than, that they offer some possible beginning of what is needed.[7]

[7] Some ways of pushing on from the elementary Austrian method, which is all that in this place I could find room to describe, are considered in chapter XII of *Capital and Time*, that entitled 'Ways Ahead'.

APPENDIX: OPTIMUM SAVING

Is it possible to say anything useful, on purely theoretical grounds, about the proportion of income which an economy should ideally save? In particular, does it depend upon the rate of return which is to be expected from those savings? These are tempting questions, but I think I can show that there is not much to be said about them in the way they have usually been discussed.

The problem is one of optimum, not actual, behaviour. It has therefore appeared to be appropriate to discuss it under the assumptions (1) that what will happen, as the result of one course of behaviour or another, can be accurately foreseen, (2) that the rate of return can be sufficiently represented by a single rate of interest, and (3) that the behaviour is that of a representative 'consumer', so that questions of distribution do not arise. One may have doubts about each of these assumptions, but they will not here be questioned. Suppose we grant them, what can we say?

It is natural to take it that our 'consumer' has an indifference map of the usual type, between consumption now and consumption in future periods. Since the dating of the consumption is all that concerns us, the consumption of each period can be represented by a single index, so much 'value'. Let ξ_t be the consumption, so reckoned, that is planned for period t. Then at time 0, he chooses a *plan*

$$(\xi_0, \xi_1, \ldots \xi_t \ldots), \text{ or simply } (\xi).$$

It must, since he chooses it, be preferred, or at least indifferent, to any other plan which is available to him.

If r is the rate of interest, $(1 + r)^{-1}$, or λ, is the discount factor. The discounted value of the stream (ξ) is

$$\xi_0 + \lambda \xi_1 + \lambda^2 \xi_2 + \ldots,$$

which I write $K(\xi, \lambda)$.

Since (ξ) is chosen at discount factor λ, any alternative plan which has a discounted value less than $K(\xi, \lambda)$ is rejected in favour of (ξ); so it is 'shown to be' on a lower 'utility' level. If $(\xi + \delta\xi)$ is on the same utility level as (ξ), it cannot be among those which are so rejected. Thus, as between two indifferent positions, we must have the Samuelson inequality

$$K(\xi + \delta\xi, \lambda) \geq K(\xi, \lambda).$$

If $(\xi + \delta\xi)$ were that actually chosen at $\lambda + \delta\lambda$, it would similarly follow that

$$K(\xi + \delta\xi, \lambda + \delta\lambda) \leq K(\xi, \lambda + \delta\lambda).$$

It then follows from this pair of Samuelson inequalities (dividing one by the other, as is permissible since all the sums are positive) that the effect of a rise in the discount factor (or a fall in the rate of interest) is in the direction of *diminishing* the ratio

$$K(\xi, \lambda + \delta\lambda)/K(\xi, \lambda)$$

If the change in the discount factor is small, this reduces to

$$1 + P(\delta\lambda/\lambda)$$

where P is an index of the *trend growth rate*[1] of the stream (ξ). So a fall in the rate of interest (a rise in λ) diminishes this growth rate. As between two indifferent positions, a rise in the rate of interest tends to increase the trend growth rate of the stream of consumptions.

. That is all that follows from the Samuelson inequalities, as so far stated; it does not tell us very much. For consider how it applies to the comparison of steady states. In a steady state, the growth rates of all elements are equal to g; so the growth rates of all the ξs are equal to g, and that of K must also be equal to g. The increase in K, from period to period, equals gK. Income by definition equals rK; so if s is the proportion of income saved, $s = gr$. All that we have learned, from the proposition so far established, is that g will be larger the larger is r; but we cannot conclude from that s increases with r. s may rise or fall, or remain constant; the only thing that is ruled out is that s should fall so much (when r increases) that sr is diminished. And even this is only ruled out so long as we confine our attention to the substitution effect. There does not seem to be any reason why we should not have, on occasion, to include an 'income' effect, which would work àn exception, even to our very weak proposition.

———————

It must have been for some such reason as this that several writers on the theory of interest and saving (from Fisher and Ramsey[2] to Tinbergen and

---

[1] P is the elasticity of $K(\xi, \lambda)$ with respect to λ. Written in full, it is

$$\Sigma t\lambda^t \xi_t / \Sigma \lambda^t \xi_t$$

Thus, unlike other elasticities, it is not a pure number, but (as a consequence of compound interest) it has the dimension of time. When I first introduced it, in *Value and Capital* (1939), pp. 186–8, I called it the *Average Period* of the stream, for I wanted to show that it is the proper generalization of the Average Period which appeared in the work of Böhm-Bawerk and in the early work of Hayek. I did, however, go on to point out in a footnote that there is a simple relation between it and what I there called the *crescendo* of the stream, what I would now prefer to call the trend growth rate. 'The best numerical definition for the crescendo of a stream of values is the rate of expansion of a stream, continuously expanding by the same proportion in every period, which has the same average period as the original stream. This rate of expansion is related to the average period by a simple formula' (p. 188).

It is easy to show that the Average Period of a stream with constant growth rate g^*, extending into an indefinite future, is $1/(r - g^*)$. Since r, the rate of interest, is here only used for purposes of computation, we should keep it unchanged when comparing one stream with another. Thus a rise in P will always correspond to a rise in g^*.

[2] Irving Fisher, *Rate of Interest* (1907), *Theory of Interest* (1930); F. Ramsey, 'Mathematical Theory of Saving' (*Economic Journal*, 1928).

Frisch[3]) have sought to specify the utility function further. Are there any particular characteristics which we may assume for the utility function plausible enough to be reasonable in most (if not all) intertemporal utility problems, and strong enough to give more definite rules about behaviour? There is a particular form of function, which has emerged from their work, and which is thought to satisfy these requirements. Certainly it does give a much stronger theory, if it is acceptable. It is tempting (and eminent economists, from Ramsey onwards, have succumbed to the temptation) to use it for making prescriptions about saving—for laying down rules of behaviour about saving, which (it is held) a rational community ought to follow. The belief that there are such rules (and that they have, at least, some degree of authority) has spread widely among economists; it is not without influence even on those who are unacquainted with the details of the Ramsey theory. The assumptions upon which the theory is based should therefore be given a close examination. I believe that I can show that they are in fact very fragile—much too fragile to stand the weight that has been put upon them.

For the simplest form of the theory we need *three* special assumptions; it will be convenient to begin by setting it out on that basis. Not all of these assumptions, we shall subsequently find, are essential, but there is one that is essential—the whole theory collapses without it. And there is a quite simple reason why that assumption is very hard to accept. It is therefore not suprising (as we shall also find) that the theory itself has some odd features; not all of the consequences that must be drawn from it make as good sense as they should. But it will be best to let all these points appear as we proceed on the basis of the three assumptions.

(1) The first of the three assumptions is *stationariness* (as Koopmans[4] has called it). This 'stationariness', it must be emphasized, is a pure characteristic of the utility function; it has nothing (necessarily) to do with Stationary Equilibrium. What it means is that the (intertemporal) want-system remains unchanged over time; as time moves forward, the whole want-system moves forward with it. More precisely, the marginal rate of substitution, between consumption t_1 periods *hence* and consumption t_2 periods *hence*, remains the same at whatever date the choice between the two consumptions is made, provided that all the planned consumptions (dated so many periods *hence*) remain the same. Consumptions are valued according to their distance in time from the planning date, whatever the planning date may be. The stationariness assumption is that the system of wants is of this character, and that the plan chosen is one that *continues* to maximize utility in terms of that want-system.

It is clearly by no means necessary, in a practical problem of planning, that this stationariness assumption should be valid. A simple case in which it

[3] J. Tinbergen, 'Optimum Savings' (*Econometrica*, 1960); R. Frisch, 'Dynamic Utility' (*Econometrica*, 1964).

[4] T. C. Koopmans, 'Stationary Ordinal Utility and Impatience' (*Econometrica*, 1960). As will be evident, I owe a great debt to this subtle paper.

would not be valid would occur with a plan which incorporated an extension of education, which will modify (and is expected to modify) the wants of the community as time goes on. But the existence of exceptions does not prevent the stationariness assumption from being an interesting assumption. It is not this assumption which I want to criticize. What is the effect of assuming stationariness is one of the questions in this field to which we should certainly like an answer.

If the stationariness assumption (and nothing else) is incorporated into our analysis by Samuelson inequalities, we shall have to add to the inequalities (written above) which compare values discounted back to time 0, similar inequalities with values discounted back to each future date (only the consumptions subsequent to that date being included in each case). The plans will in fact have to be tested for indifference *all along the line*. Manipulating these in the same manner as before, we shall find that the substitution effect (of a rise in the rate of interest) must not only increase the trend growth rate of the whole stream

$$(\xi_0, \xi_1, \xi_2, \xi_3, \xi_4, \ldots);$$

it must also increase the trend growth rates of the remainder-streams

$$(\xi_1, \xi_2, \xi_3, \xi_4, \ldots)$$
$$(\xi_2, \xi_3, \xi_4, \ldots)$$

and so on. This of course a stronger condition than that with which we started. But it does not, by itself, overcome the crucial weakness of the original proposition. For if we apply it, as before, to the comparison of constant growth paths, it tells us no more than the first pair of Samuelson inequalities did. If the paths under comparison are constant growth rate paths, the trend growth rates of the remainder streams will be the same as that of the original stream; so that if one condition is satisfied, all are satisfied. Taken by itself, the stationariness assumption gets us hardly any further.

(2) The second assumption to be introduced is *homogeneity*. What is meant by this is the same as what is meant by homogeneity in the case of the homogeneous production function—an increase in consumptions (inputs) in the same proportion will increase utility (output) in a proportion that depends upon the utility (output) level, but is independent of the proportions in which the consumptions (inputs) are combined. Homogeneity of the utility function does not imply cardinality; it is a pure property of the indifference curves (or surfaces). Here, if (ξ) and (ξ') are two streams that are on the same indifference level, we are to get another pair of indifferent streams when we multiply every item in (ξ) and every item in (ξ') by any identical multiplier. It follows from this property that the marginal rate of substitution, between consumption at time t_1 and consumption at time t_2, is entirely determined by the *ratios* between consumptions at these and at other dates. Consequently, if the rate of interest (which plays the part of a price system) is given, the ratios

between planned consumptions (at different dates) will be determined, irrespective of the general level of consumption that is attainable over the whole sequence. So long as the rate of interest remains unchanged, an increase in total wealth will increase planned consumption, in all periods, in the same proportion.

In itself, this homogeneity assumption looks harmless; it amounts to no more than a bracketing together of 'income' and substitution effect; the 'income effect' is made manageable by being reduced to the simplest form that it can possibly take. But when this assumption is combined with the stationariness assumption, the result is drastic.

If the want-system is stationary, and is also homogeneous, the only type of consumption plan that can be optimal, at a constant rate of interest, is a plan with a constant growth rate. For if

$$(\xi_0, \xi_1, \xi_2, \dots)$$

the optimum plan at time 0, and

$$(\xi_1, \xi_2, \dots)$$

the optimum plan at time 1, are plans that maximize utility under the same want-system (stationariness), the only difference between them (when the rate of interest is constant) must be such as arise from the change in capital value, due to saving that has occurred (or that may have occurred) in the period 0 to 1. If such a change in capital value changes all consumptions in the same proportion (homogeneity), it will follow at once that

$$\xi_1/\xi_0 = \xi_2/\xi_1 = \xi_3/\xi_2 = \dots$$

so that the growth rate of consumption must be constant, from period to period. Only a constant growth rate plan can be chosen (at constant rate of interest) if there is stationariness and there is also homogeneity.

There is certainly no question that this is a convenient property, and to reach it in this way may perhaps persuade us to adopt it with a lighter heart. But even if we do accept it, it does not, in itself, give us any help in dealing with the problem with which we began. For it was precisely in relation to constant growth rate paths that our original difficulty came up most sharply. All that can be said, even when we have both of these first two assumptions, is that a rise in the rate of interest will tend to increase the growth rate of the optimum path—our former propostion, only made a little more precise, since we need no longer talk about 'trends' and have absorbed the old reservation about income effects. But the effect on the proportion of income saved remains as obscure as ever.

(3) The third assumption is that of *independence*. This is the point at which we go over to Cardinal Utility; but it is not the cardinality that is important—it is the independence which is taken to go with it. A general assumption of cardinality would itself impose no additional restriction; but there is an

additional restriction when the cardinal utility function is assumed to take the particular form of a sum of *separated* utilities

$$U_0(\xi_0) + U_1(\xi_1) + U_2(\xi_2) + \ldots$$

so that the marginal utility of consumption in each single period is taken to depend upon consumption in that particular single period *only*. A cardinal measure of that particular form does imply an ordinal property: the marginal rate of substitution between consumption at time t_1 and consumption at time t_2 (being the ratio between the marginal utilities of these consumptions) is made to depend upon these two consumptions only; consumptions at other dates do not affect it. If we have that ordinal property, it must be possible to put the utility function (if we choose to do so) into the form which has just been given;[5] if we can have the separated form, we must have the ordinal property. The two are strictly equivalent.

It is independence (in this sense) which, when added to the other assumptions, works the transformation. The consequences of the combination are very far-reaching indeed.

Take homogeneity and independence together. Homogeneity says that all consumptions are to increase in the same proportion when there is a change in capital value (and no change in interest); independence says that the marginal utilities of the consumptions (which are to keep the same proportions to one another since there is no change in interest) are each of them dependent upon its own consumption only. These things can only happen together if all of the (separated) marginal utility curves have the same elasticity; and since we might have started from any combination of consumptions, they must have the same elasticities at all points of the curves, which can only happen if each curve is a curve of constant elasticity—the same constant elasticity for each separated curve. Thus the marginal utility of consumption at time t must be given by the fomula

$$q_t \xi_t^{-(1/\eta)}$$

where η is the (common) constant elasticity, and q_t is a constant, that may vary from one curve to another.

At an optimum position, this is to be proportional to the discount factor, which we have been writing as λ^t. In this case, however, it is neater to work with continuous time. Let us accordingly write the discount factor as e^{-rt}, where r is (now) an *instantaneous* rate of interest. It follows at once that ξ_t must be proportional to

$$q_t^\eta e^{\eta rt}$$

---

[5] That the correspondence works both ways is becoming familiar through the use that is being made of the independence assumption in other connexions, by such writers as R. H. Strotz, 'The Utility Tree' (*Econometrica*, 1957), and I. F. Pearce, *A Contribution to Demand Analysis* (1964).

We must have a consumption path (at the optimum) such as can be represented by this formula, if there is to be homogeneity and also independence.

If there is also to be stationariness, the path must be a constant growth path; and this formula will only give a constant growth path if q_t itself has a constant rate of growth (or decline) over time. Now the qs are the weights that are given to future utilities to make them comparable with present; it follows from the stationariness assumption that these weights can only differ because of delay (as t increases). It is commonly accepted that the delay will diminish the (present) utility of future consumptions; let us grant that (at least provisionally). We may therefore write $q_t = Ce^{-pt}$, where p is to be constant (the rate of time-preference). Finally, therefore, we have

$$\xi_t = C^\eta e^{\eta(r-p)t}$$

so that the growth rate of the consumption stream emerges as

$$g = \eta(r-p)$$

an elegant formula which (it appears) is due to Champernowne.[6] In so far as this formula is acceptable, it is undoubtedly more informative than the bare rule that the bare rule that the growth rate rises with the rate of interest, with which we started.

But is it acceptable? Let us begin by noticing some of its implications.

The familiar $g = sr$ is still valid (along a constant growth path) even though we are using instantaneous rates.[7] Thus, for the proportion of income saved, we have (from the Champernowne formula)

$$s = \eta\left(1 - \frac{p}{r}\right)$$

from which there immediately follow the Ramsey properties: (1) that if there is no time-preference ($p = 0$) we have $s = \eta$, so that the proportion of income saved is independent of the rate of interest; (2) if p is positive, there will be zero saving when $r = p$, while if $r > p$, the saving-proportion will be larger, the larger r, up to a maximum at $s = \eta$, as before. These are quite sharp conclusions; but they are odd conclusions. The more one reflects upon them, the odder they seem.

It must surely be supposed that consumption must always be positive; $s < 1$. But it has just been shown that if $p = 0$, $s = \eta$; so that the model will only make sense, when $p = 0$, if $\nu < 1$; the marginal utility curves must be *inelastic*. If $p > 0$, we can have $s < 1$, with $\eta < 1$, if the rate of interest is not too high; but we shall find consumption going negative at high rates of interest. This is

[6] According to D. H. Robertson, *Lectures on Economic Principles*, vol. ii, p. 79.

[7] It will be remembered that we are not distinguishing between profits and wages; capital value is the discounted value of the whole stream of consumptions; income is the interest on this capital value.

intolerable; it must therefore be concluded (and has been concluded in fact by Ramsey and his followers) that we must take $\eta < 1$. But there is no intuitive reason why the marginal utility curves should be inelastic; it is odd[8] that we should have to make them inelastic in order to make sense of the theory.

It further follows that if the marginal utility curves are inelastic, the total utility function (for the individual dated consumption) must be such that there is a limit beyond which utility cannot rise however much consumption increases; utility cannot increase indefinitely. Ramsey's 'Bliss' is an essential character of the model; the whole construction depends upon it. But (again) it is not obvious intuitively why the utility function must have this property.

There is a final point, which was not noticed by Ramsey.[9] If the utility function, $U_t(\xi_t)$, for the individual dated consumption must have this form, the utility of the whole stream, which is the sum of $U_t(\xi_t)$ from $t = 0$ to $t =$ infinity, will not be finite unless $p > 0$. But it is the total utility, in the sense of this sum, which is being maximized. One cannot maximize something which is infinite. So that unless $p > 0$, the whole construction breaks down.

Thus it is not fair to proceed as Ramsey did, to treat zero time-preference as a criterion for rationality, and to pour scorn upon the weakness of our telescopic vision which makes us unwilling to save at the high rates which (it is alleged) would be appropriate for $p = 0$. If there is no time-preference, then (on the theory) it is necessary that the curves should be inelastic; but if the curves are inelastic, it is impossible that $p = 0$.

What has happened? We must go back to the assumptions and look at them again. One which is clearly weak is homogeneity. Can we drop that, and get something that is more acceptable?

If we drop homogeneity, but maintain stationariness, we shall drop the constant growth path. But perhaps it is that which ought to be abandoned.

If we drop homogeneity, but maintain independence, we are not tied down to a particular utility function; we can give the marginal utility curves another form. Quite general forms are hard to handle; but there is one (which was considered by Ramsey) which is quite simple, and which is surely an improvement. This would make the marginal utility of consumption become infinite, not at zero consumption, but at some positive 'subsistence' level. We can then keep something like the 'constant elasticity' form, but shift the whole curve to the right. That is to say, for the marginal utility of consumption at time t, we should have

$$q_t(\xi_t - A)^{-(1/\eta)}$$

which would give

$$\xi_t = A + Ce^{\eta(r-p)t}$$

[8] As Tinbergen has noticed (op. cit.).
[9] I owe it to the paper by Koopmans, where it is established in much more general terms.

if we stick to the constant rate of time-preference. The result is thus that it is not consumption as a whole, but the excess of consumption over subsistence, which has the constant growth rate, the rate that is given by the Champernowne formula.

It can be shown that if g is this growth rate, the proportion of income saved (at time t) is given by

$$\frac{S_t}{1-S_t} = \frac{g}{r-g} \left(1-\frac{A}{\xi_t}\right).$$

If (as we may suppose) consumption rises with time, this gives the proportion of income saved rising with time, being low when consumption (and therefore income) is low, but rising towards a limit, which is the same limit as was expressed by the former formula

$$s = (g/r) = \eta \left(1-\frac{p}{r}\right).$$

Thus if we begin with a level of income that is near subsistence, there is no difficulty in admitting low rates of saving; but the same difficulties (essentially the same difficulties as before) emerge at high levels of income. An amendment of this kind does not seem to be much help; and it looks probable that the same sort of thing would happen if we changed over to any other plausible marginal utility function.

What then of independence? It is more and more apparent that it is independence that is the key assumption. As long as we maintain independence we are bound to get something like the Ramsey results; but what is the case for the independence assumption? As soon as we face up to it, and consider (quite directly) what it implies, it becomes apparent that the case for making it is very weak indeed.

If the successive consumptions (ξ_t) have independent utilities, the amount of present consumption which the chooser will be willing to give up, in order to be able to increase consumption in year 5 from so much to so much, will be independent of the consumptions that are planned for years 4 and 6. It will be just the same, whether the increase in year 5 is to be a sudden spurt, out of line with its neighbours, or if it is needed to fill a gap, to make up a deficiency (that would otherwise have occurred in year 5), so raising the consumption of year 5 up to the common level. This is what is implied by the independence assumption; when it is stated in those terms, surely it must be said that it cannot be accepted. The sacrifice which one would be willing to make to fill a gap must normally be much greater than what it would be worth while to incur for a mere extra. There is indeed a sense in which there is a rapidly falling 'marginal utility of consumption' in the particular period. But it is not due to the inelasticity of an independent 'marginal utility curve'; it is due to the complementarity between the consumption that is planned for the particular period and that which is planned for its neighbours. It is nonsense to assume that successive consumptions are independent; the normal condition is that there is a strong complementarity between them.

It is not to be denied that there are some kinds of saving which are directed towards particular future expenditures, so that the complementarity with neighbouring consumptions may for them be rather weak. But the clearest case of this is saving for a particular event (as for one's own old age, or for the marriage of one's children); and though there may be independence in these instances, it is abundantly clear that with them the stationariness assumption will not hold. Even with them we do not have independence and stationariness. Other sorts of saving-up, as for the purchase of durable consumer-goods (in the days before consumer credit) are not, I think, exceptions to the rule of complementarity.

Any saving which is not just saving-up—saving which is a pure exchange of present for future satisfactions, satisfactions that are not inherently different save that the one is present and the other is future—must, because of the complementarity, take the form of the substitution, for the present consumption, of some sort of a *flow* of consumption in the future. This is, surely, how it appears to the ordinary man; this is why what is offered to him (nearly always) is interest, or dividend, or annuity, on his savings. The institutional arrangements are a practical recognition of the complementarity that is in question. Saving of this kind (and it is the only kind for which the stationariness assumption is appropriate) cannot be adequately analysed by considering the present and *one particular future date* in isolation.

What are being compared are present sacrifice, and *flow* of future satisfaction. If the complementary is perfect, so that the time-shape of the future consumption-flow is taken as fixed (and this, though an extreme assumption, is a better assumption than the assumption of independence), we can treat the planned future consumption as a single good, and represent the whole choice on a two-dimensional diagram. But it is a choice between sharply different things: once-for-all consumption in the present period, and a stream of consumption exteding into the indefinite future. Nothing more can be laid down about such a choice than we are accustomed to say about the choice between any two commodities (or commodity bundles). The supply curve of saving agaisnt the rate of interest may be rising from left to right or may turn back on itself (but for nothing more than the usual Walrasian reason).

When we particularize, splitting up the stream of consumptions into particular dated items, we do not change the situation fundamentally, once we allow for the complementarity. But there can be as much complementarity as is possible, and the Samuelson inequalities will still hold. Thus we come back to the rule about a rise in the rate of interest increasing the trend growth rate—the 'poor thing' with which we started.

I should like to emphasize, in conclusion, that we get no further than this by assuming 'rationality'. If the question is simply one of the choice between two 'commodities', it is equally rational to give a high value, or a low value, to one in terms of the other. The only thing that is irrational is to act in such a way as must result in future damage, and to leave it out of calculation. Thus it is ordinarily irrational to 'waste one's substance'—to indulge in a high rate of current consumption, which must be followed, at some point, by a fall to a much lower level. Violent contractions are exceedingly painful, and it is foolish to expose oneself to such pain by lack of foresight. But as for the amount which should be sacrificed now in order to bring about a rise in the future *stream*—that is a matter on which wisdom may have more than one opinion.

INDEX